# THE AMERICAN WAY

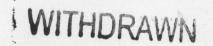

John Ise at his desk.

# THE AMERICAN WAY

JOHN ISE

*Illustrations*

*by*

SUE EPPERSON

*Published by*
MEMBERS OF THE FACULTY
*in the*
DEPARTMENT OF ECONOMICS AND SCHOOL OF BUSINESS
UNIVERSITY OF KANSAS
LAWRENCE, KANSAS

38957

PRINTED IN U.S.A. The Allen Press, Lawrence, Kansas

# Foreword

When John Ise retires from teaching at the University of Kansas, as very sadly he is soon to do, it will seem as if some unkind person had tunneled away Mount Oread itself and left the University on the dull plain.

To those of us who know John Ise or have felt his influence, KU will thereafter be a different place. We can only hope that somewhere on the campus, another authentic Kansan will hold up the same clear, candid mirror to the life about him, will press insistently the claims of reason and will continue to invoke the truly liberal spirit which admits it may not always be right.

John Ise has spent a lifetime trying to drag his native Kansas into the twentieth century. Nobody can say Kansas hasn't put up a fight. There were moments when it almost seemed that John was winning—with an assist from the depression. But farm prices went up and Kansans turned back happily to singing—strictly to each other, of course—John's favorite song: *The More We Get Together, the Happier We'll Be.*

The same mail that brought me the essays in this book with their happy freight of memories also brought a copy of a lecture delivered at the Kansas Centennial Conference at the University on April 30, 1954, by the distinguished historian, Allan Nevins, who wrote the magnificent *Ordeal of the Union.* He had entitled it "Kansas and the Stream of American Destiny."

Mr. Nevins examined with professional detachment the relations between the hundred-year career of Kansas and the parallel career of the whole republic. He found that in their respective careers they had followed "highly divergent roads" and that "national destiny and State destiny have in large degree lain crosswise."

It seemed to me that with all his polished prose, Mr. Nevins was prey to an uneasy feeling that he wasn't being quite nice. Why, shucks, Professor, compared to what John Ise has been giving Kansas with the bark off all these years, your cadenced rhetoric was a lullaby!

The inner security which permits John Ise to raise the right questions is matched by a brain which makes them the right questions.

After I had returned from a stint of war correspondence, I found myself seated at dinner next to a professor of economics from Bowdoin College in Maine, one of the select company of admired small colleges in our country. "Believe it or not, you see before you an economics major," I told him. "What texts are you using?"

"We think, and many colleges agree with us, that we have the best economics text," he replied. "Oddly enough, it comes from Kansas . . . ."

Throwing Emily Post to the winds, I interrupted. I was right, of course. John Ise wrote that text.

I pass over that phrase "oddly enough." When I went east to work I became accustomed to the question: "What was your college?" Meaning of course, did I go to Vassar, Mount Holyoke, Bryn Mawr or Smith. I always answered haughtily, "College? I went to a University." Then I moved away before they could ask me how long it had been since Oxford admitted women.

The fact is that I went to that kind of ideal university which was in President Garfield's mind when he said that the ideal university was a log with a boy at one end and Mark Hopkins at the other.

Fortunately for me, KU is co-educational, and fortunately also, John Ise was at the other end of my log.

DORIS FLEESON, K.U., '23

*In honor of John Ise*
*on the occasion of his retirement from active teaching*
*at the University of Kansas,*
*a selection of his speeches and letters*
*is published in this book*
*by the members of the faculty*
*in the Department of Economics*
*and the School of Business.*

# CONTENTS

# THE AMERICAN WAY

*What Ford has accomplished for automobiles, the fraternities
have done for our college output.*

# IN DEFENSE OF FRATERNITIES

*An address delivered on Honors Day at Iowa State College, May 24, 1945. Complete and unexpurgated.*

Doubtless the earliest reference to college fraternities is found in Plato's "Republic" where Plato classified men into gold, silver and copper; and it speaks strongly for the vitality of the American Ideal that this germ of an idea, expressed casually more than two thousand years ago while America was yet a wilderness, should have grown and blossomed into thousands of fraternities and sororities with hundreds of thousands of brothers and sisters. Perhaps no other American institution has so completely met the needs and aspirations of so many people.

Yet there are men and women who criticize these institutions. The great Thorstein Veblen, in an unfortunate lapse from his usual perspicacity, spoke of college fraternities as "an expression of that heritage of clannishness which is so large a feature in the temperament of the predatory barbarian." There are others who insist that fraternities ruin the democracy that should prevail in our so-called educational institutions, that they develop an unfortunate snobbishness on the part of the members and an inferiority complex in those outside, that they divert to social activities energy and interest that should be devoted to books and class work, that they set up standards of wealth and luxury where intellectual standards should prevail. There are even some who object to what they consider the standardizing tendencies of fraternity life.

It should be admitted without argument that fraternities are not democratic institutions in the ordinary sense. In almost all colleges and universities there are fraternities of different grades or qualities. The first grade includes four or five of the oldest and wealthiest organizations enrolling the academic cream, the Brahmins, so to speak. These may be designated as the socially A prime, choice heavy. Grade two includes those of somewhat lesser wealth and position, yet of reasonably high quality—the socially medium heavy to choice. Grade three, fair to medium, includes in its membership those who have social ambitions but are unable to make the higher grades. The lower grades have generally smaller houses and smaller mortgages than the higher grades, but there are exceptions to this rule. Outside all fraternities is the great body of the social proletariat, the unwashed and unanointed barbarians—vulgarly called "barbs" in academic parlance.

In a properly co-ordinated fraternity system the different grades of fraternities are mutually exclusive—that is to say, the members of each grade associate only with those within the same grade; they are forbidden to consort with those in the lower grades; and, of course, they cannot generally associate much with those in the higher grades. Courtship and marriage outside a given grade are considered forms of miscegenation and are generally punished by various forms of torture, perhaps including loss of fraternity pins and privileges. This is not universally true, to be sure, for in some colleges and universities the social life, like life on the western frontier a generation ago, is relatively simple and not well-organized. The better classes do not usually send their children to such institutions so there is little need for fraternities.

Nothing speaks more eloquently of the fraternal spirit of these organizations than the fact that they often pledge young men and women who lack the social graces that characterize their membership—the sons and daughters of former members who have contributed to the building fund. Such young men and women sometimes present very serious problems indeed. They may have bowlegs or broken arches, may be subject to melancholia or moral astigmatism; they may dance awkwardly, or perhaps even prefer to read or play ping pong; or they may lean toward undignified friendships with the academic proletarians. Yet so strong is the spirit of brotherhood among true Greeks that they will admit such social mavericks and devote years to their reclamation. In the long run this usually proves a wise policy, for such biological sports, although themselves of apparently poor endowments, are likely to have superior children who in the next generation will return to Alpha Alpha Alpha and maintain its highest social traditions. In the long run blood will tell. Even while they are in school, the social misfits are less embarrassing to their brothers and sisters than the outside world is likely to imagine for they are usually required to join a very interesting group within the fraternity known as the "cellar gang" who, on important occasions when it is necessary for the fraternity to appear at its best, are permitted to eat in the cellar with the help. All successful fraternities have cellar gangs.

Thus, fraternities are exclusive—snobbish, if you insist. Their purpose is to provide homes for the better classes of students where they will not be brought too much into contact with those less favorably endowed. But can there be any objection to that? College should be a preparation for life; and the student who learns to imitate and, if possible, to cultivate those above him, to fraternize with those on his own level, and to ignore those below him, has learned one of the most useful lessons that a college can teach, a lesson that will smooth the way for his advancement forever afterward. If he would succeed out in the world, he must look up and not down, must cultivate those on his own level or, if possible, those above him—they are the ones who can do him the most good. If he learns to worship wealth, he is saved from the danger of questioning the motives or character of those who largely control our destinies. A critical attitude toward wealth or men of wealth is an almost fatal handicap in the race of life. The business employee must always speak well of the boss; the journalist must write the language the proprietor wishes written; the lawyer must serve his rich clients; the professor must hold views acceptable to wealthy trustees and donors. Those who kowtow to wealth shall inherit the earth—or whatever portion of it the rich do not have nailed down. Shakespeare, a very eminent English writer, with a clear appreciation of life's realities, put this fundamental truth clearly in his play, *Hamlet*:

[6]

"For what advancement may I hope from thee
That no revenue hast but thy good spirits
To feed and clothe thee? Why should the poor
    be flatter'd?
No, let the candied tongue lick absurd pomp,
And crook the pregnant hinges of the knee
Where thrift may follow fawning."

Shakespeare wrote of life as it is, not of life as it would, could or should be.

It might be urged that snubbing those below is not equally advantageous; yet, it is not certain that it is a habit to be discouraged. There is little to be gained in cultivating those of small means and influence. They can seldom do us any good. Time and energy devoted to them may always be spent more profitably in cultivating the good graces of those above us. Even a snobbish attitude and demeanor—or let us say an attitude of conscious superiority—if not too crude and obvious, may often prove an asset. Most successful people have it, and men make no mistake by aping the successful—or there would not be a hundred million Americans doing it. Cultivation of graceful snobbery is training for life.

Many professorial idealists would try to build up an artificial un-American democracy in our colleges; but this would not train our young people for life; nor would it be a healthy society. Every society must have its aristocracy, its superiors and inferiors, its have's and its have not's. It is only in such a society that life can have real zest. The example of Russia shows how drab and uninteresting can be a society of equals. Surely we are not to train our young people for life in Russia!

It has been suggested that there should be colleges

specially adapted to the socially fit students where poorer students would not be admitted—where the blue blood could flow pure and uncontaminated. This proposal, however, ignores the fact that there would be none to be superior to in such a college; and much of the value of fraternity membership would be lacking. As in the world outside, there must be superior and inferior people—according to the Einstein principle of relativity—to give superiority its proper meaning.

The common fraternity ban on friendships and marriages with those of inferior grades, although often subject to criticism, is a mere rule of common sense. It is the rule of the great world about us and of good society everywhere. Nowhere is it the custom for daughters of bankers or of captains of industry to marry soda squirts or bartenders or chauffeurs or preachers or professors. Such misalliances are always regarded as scandalous, worthy of at least a column in the daily tabloid. There is no reason why friendships and marriages which violate good taste and convention in the outside world should be sanctioned in the university. Academic registration and enrollment cannot greatly alter the social qualities of young men and women and cannot be a certification of social fitness as long as the lower classes are admitted freely to our institutions of learning. Friendships are far more likely to be mutually satisfying between equals, anyhow; and marriages of those of unequal status are almost invariably disastrous.

It is not even known to what extent such morganatic marriages are likely to prove fertile, since the biological laws of hybridization are not yet well understood. Huxley cites the well-authenticated instance of a Pi Phi girl who married a member of a grade-three professional and bore two children. One of the children was pigeon-toed, and the other developed hay fever at an early age. In his exhaustive study of hybrids and mongrels, Steinberg mentions the case of a Beta who married a girl whose only distinction was a Phi Beta Kappa key. She had three children, physically normal but all introverts and all allergic to education. Robertson, whose study of this question is doubtless the best available, mentions several similar cases—one case of a Sigma Chi who married a female barbarian to whom were born four healthy children, apparently normal in all respects. Since such morganatic unions are very rare, there is far less well-tested evidence than we need for a scientific conclusion in the matter; and granting that such unions may be fertile, there is still the possibility that the children of such unions, like hybrids and mongrels generally, may themselves be barren or that hidden weaknesses or abnormalities may appear in later generations. In several cases recorded by Robertson, such children showed definite abnormalities: adenoids, cross eyes, flat feet, warts, and various types of complexes. This problem would not seem so serious if it were known that the fraternity blue blood, the fraternity chromosomes, were the dominant characters; but here again, the scientists are not yet certain of their conclusions.

Such marriages could seldom prove happy anyhow. Such a family would have no definite social status. The children would find themselves ostracized by former friends of the more eligible parent, and yet they could hardly be expected to find really satisfactory companionship with the associates of the plebeian father or mother. In some respects their situation would scarcely be preferable to that of illegitimate children. It is perhaps better to have one parent unknown than to know who he is and that he is not what he should be.

It is unfortunate, to be sure, that the social poise and polish to be gained by fraternity life go to those who, coming from homes of refinement and culture, need it least while those who come to college with the hay in their hair and the aroma of the barnyard on their feet enjoy few opportunities for the cultivation of social grace. Yet this is quite in accord with the biblical principle which governs economic and social life everywhere: Unto everyone that hath shall be given, but from him that hath not shall be taken away even that which he was about to get. It is surely not a fault of the fraternities that they conform to one of the laws of God.

Many of these proletarian young men and women have been reared in homes of little dignity or distinction. Their parents are largely people, honorable no doubt but of the lower middle class, who live by vulgarly productive work in which the children take part. In such homes, the fathers do not generally do much fishing or hunting, perhaps do not even play golf, but go to church on Sunday mornings instead. Many of them have no dogs and know nothing of mixing cocktails. Even the mothers, often with more than two children, work a great deal since they have no maids; and so they generally miss the cultural influences of the bridge, study and uplift clubs. There can, of course, be little refinement in such homes; and the children reared there have their manners and habits so firmly fixed before they enter college that they would have great difficulty in adjusting themselves to the atmosphere of a fraternity even if their natural endowments were of sufficiently high character.

*In Defense of Fraternities*

The same professors who envision an ideal of social and financial democracy in our colleges are the most ardent advocates of another type of aristocracy—an aristocracy of intellect and what they delight in calling "culture." These professors try to fence off exclusive intellectual cliques represented by honor rolls, Phi Beta Kappa, Coif and Sigma Xi with appropriate initiation ceremonies, with banquets and learned addresses and with emblems of keys and badges. If the professors had their way, we should, no doubt, have students classified into exclusive groups, "rated" according to grades, class attendance, intelligence quotients, knowledge of ancient philosophers, appreciation of Homer, Goethe, Bach, Beethoven, or other celebrities dead at least a century. No doubt, lovers of Bach would snub the lovers of Beethoven who would, in turn, turn up their noses at the lovers of Schubert, while the low devotees of jazz would enter buildings by the back doors. Presumably, students in philosophy, Greek and Latin would stand at the top of the social hierarchy since such studies are more clearly useless in the preparation of young men and women for real life than any others in the college curriculum. In the view of most professors, only such studies as are far removed from the realities of life have genuine worth and dignity.

Only a moment's reflection is necessary to reveal that an aristocracy of intellect and culture would be far more cruel and further removed from the sweet ideal of democracy than the present pecuniary aristocracy of the fraternities. There are few students indeed who could rise to intellectual aristocracy even by the most arduous application. In no college could as many as 5 per cent of the students be classified as intellectual aristocrats by

[ 11 ]

any stretch of the imagination. There are always a great many students, on the other hand, who can learn to wash their necks and put on a semblance of prosperity. In some colleges, half of the students belong to fraternities. From this point of view, fraternities are truly democratic institutions; and their social aristocracy is far less offensive to people generally than any sort of intellectual aristocracy would be. The pecuniary aristocracy of the fraternities has the vast advantage, finally, that it can be paid for by the parents while intellectual quality would have to be earned by the students themselves, at a heavy sacrifice in their opportunities for pleasure and recreation. The parents are happy in working their children's way through the fraternities for that is their chief ambition in life; and the children are happy to see them do it. Thus, parents and children are both happy as the business works now, while a system of intellectual and cultural aristocracy would answer the aspirations of neither.

There is, furthermore, a strong element of equity in our system of pecuniary caste. The social aristocrats have the social esteem with which they are entirely happy. Many of them, if they had not that, would have little indeed; and their lives would be most "stale, flat and unprofitable." The intellectuals can enjoy their lucubration, their philosophy and literature, their comradeship with erudite professors. They can enjoy their culture for its own sake. It would be cruel and unjust indeed to give all prestige to the small minority who have the capacity and the inclination to learn their lessons.

The assumption that fraternities train only for snobbery would be a grave error, for social stratification demands, from another angle, a proper sense of deference and humility. Only the members of a very few of the highest groups can be superior to all; the others are inferior to these just as they are in turn superior to others. Excepting the highest of the Brahmins, all are in a sense inferiors as well as superiors and must learn the ways of humility with whatever grace they may command. In this social hierarchy, all must learn their places; and in doing so, they learn a lesson of profound importance for their later advancement in the practical world.

The charge that fraternities do not emphasize scholarship is perhaps justly made, but is it really a damning accusation? Naturally, college faculties would like to see the students devote themselves religiously to their studies. Many professors think that the courses offered are the most important things about a college, that studying is the most important function of the students, that those who can be coaxed or cajoled into a respectful attitude toward Homer and Virgil and Shakespeare and Adam Smith are on the way to being educated. But the fact is that the courses and the curricula of our colleges do not train for real life, for the happy hurly-burly of American business. Indeed, it is difficult to imagine worse preparation for life than a thorough training in philosophy or literature. Imagine the philosopher promoting a new corporation, selling the stock to practical men, or indeed trying to sell anything to anybody! Let him quote Kant and Hegel and Spinoza—what will it avail him? Imagine him in the mazes of Wall Street, in the busy mart, in the counting house, at the Rotary Club, or at the bridge table, or at the night club! He would not only be a failure but a bore and a nuisance everywhere. Who has not seen the angry glances directed at the idiot who insists on talking philosophy, literature or economics when he should be attending to his cards or at the highbrow who turns the radio to the philharmonic concert when he might have found Amos 'n Andy on a dozen wave lengths. I once saw such a person empty the lounge room of the university commons of a hundred students in five minutes by exactly such conduct.

No, the philosophers, the students of literature, the devotees of the cult of learning are unfit for every important function of our society unless it be to teach others the philosophy or literature that has ruined them. Hundreds of red-blooded young men, full of the vitality and enthusiasm needed in the great world of business, itching for a chance to enter the lists in the battle for profits, are ruined every year in our colleges and universities. After four years of rhetoric, literature, philosophy, history and economics, they enter a world which has little use for any of these but demands the fresh enthusiasm and the unquestioning zeal which, in these students, has ebbed with every accumulation of college credits and has given place to doubts and uncertainties. Out in the world, when they should be hitting the line, they wonder whether hitting the line is the most important thing or whether something else might be of more genuine worth. The more they have absorbed of curricular learning, the more they are likely to wonder and philosophize; and, of course, the time and energy devoted to wondering and philosophizing cannot be devoted to sales promotion. The students who have taken their studies seriously are handicapped throughout their later life, if they are engaged in business, and are beaten at every turn by the men who have devoted their precious energies to learning the ways of the world.

College education in America is an anachronism anyhow, so strange that we would scarcely believe any such business possible were we not calloused to its absurdities by long familiarity. Young men and women, many of them the children of able and successful parents—bankers, lawyers, salesmen, organizers, captains of industry, congressmen, bootleggers—at college studying under sexless professors of both sexes who, likely as not, have to write papers, make speeches and keep roomers to eke out a living! I have actually seen boys in college, the sons of men earning fifty thousand a year, studying business under professors of finance who had to wear their shirts three days to save laundry bills! By the unmistakable criterion of their incomes, professors are condemned as either incompetent or as hopeless devotees of the cult of "learning"; and in either case they are not inspiring leaders for the young men and women who wish to learn of life as it is lived.

The tendency toward standardization of dress, of conduct and of ideals, which is so often mentioned as one of the unfortunate consequences of fraternity life is really one of its greatest contributions to American culture.

Members of each fraternity enforce standardization within the group as far as possible. Members must all wear collars acceptably, comb their hair in much the same way, using the same grease. It is often possible to classify fraternities by smell. The Betas have long had a preference for violet, the Sigma Chis for jasmine, the Alpha Taus for heliotrope, the Phi Gams for attar of roses and the Phi Phis for attar of corn and hops. All members must behave alike—must properly observe the social amenities and cultivate a similarly blasé attitude toward all things, for evidence of interest is, of course, the unmistakable sign of the roughneck.

Standardization applies not only to those in each fraternity but to the members of all fraternities in a given social grade and, since all fraternity members ape those above them, applies to the members of all fraternities in the institution. All fraternities of importance have national chapters, too, so are able to standardize on a nation-wide scale. A Beta is Beta quality everywhere, just as No. 1 hard wheat or Armour's sausages are everywhere the same. Furthermore, since college barbarians tend to copy the social leaders, we may say that we have a fairly effective standardization of all American college students. This standardization is analogous to the great principle of exchangeable parts in industry; it is the great American contribution to society as well as to industry. What Ford has accomplished for automobiles, the fraternities have done for our college output.

There can be no denying the advantages of this. Many will recall the great service Herbert Hoover performed as head of the Commerce Department in standardizing door hinges. This not only simplified the problems of contractors and builders but reduced costs of manufacturing and selling and so contributed to the upbuilding of the great American home. Standardization, coupled with the jewelled brand which is worn by all the socially elect, constitutes a guaranty of uniform quality which is as much a convenience in social matters as the trade mark or government stamp is in business. Phi Gam, Beta, Phi Delt, Sigma Chi, Pi Phi, Theta, Kappa— do they not bring to mind the same connotation of approved and tested quality as Ivory Soap, Del Monte Canned Peas, Bond Bread or Swift's Premium Hams? I have seen strangers meet on the train, note the jewelled pin, and, confident of quality, enter into a pleasant conversation for the remainder of the journey.

Some critics object to this standardization and certification as involving a loss of individuality. It should be evident, however, that the world would move far more smoothly if all people had similar manners and ideals. Not only would our social life be simplified but also the problems of college administration, policing and instruction. Raw, rampant rugged individualism is nowhere more troublesome than in college; and in college is nowhere more troublesome than in class. Students who insist on raising questions in class are likely to disturb the smooth flow of the instructor's thought and are always irritating to the other students. Worst of all, they are likely to be troublesome nonconformists in their later lives, perhaps may be inclined to question the most fundamental institutions.

The cultural value of individuality is always overstressed by idealists. Cranks who find life's fullness in rattling around freely within the confines of their own rugged individualism always assume that other people should enjoy themselves similarly—a most absurd assumption as we may see by observing people at a football game, in a parade or at a Rotary dinner. Americans are not individualists; they like to lose themselves as completely as possible in the biggest crowd possible and yell—just as the Germans once found their emotional release in shouting *Hoch der Kaiser* or *Heil Hitler*, just as the Italians found the fullness of life in strutting for Mussolini.

Fortunately, fraternity standardization grades up and not down. The best dress, the most polished manners, the most expensive hair oil set the standard. All members learn to dress correctly—something of far more importance than all the courses given in any college; they learn to cover what is sometimes a cultural vacuum with an impenetrable shell of poise and confidence.

These well-dressed and well-mannered young men and women, with their jewelled pins, their expensive houses and cars and parties, give college life a distinction, a swanky vogue which it would never have without them—a swanky vogue like that of army officers or of the diplomatic service. Indeed, it is not certain that colleges could be maintained without them. They are the magnet that draws most students to college, not only the socially fit but many of the barbarians who hope to slip into a fraternity some time before graduation. If there were no fraternities in college, the young people from the better homes would go largely to military schools where they could wear pretty uniforms and puttees and where they would be protected from bothersome thinking, over-individualization and other forms of mental distress even more efficiently than in college.

It is to the fraternities that credit must be given for the splendid development of that other college activity—athletics. The fraternities not only bring capable athletes to colleges but often generously stable and feed them without compensation and so make possible the magnificent football teams that play on our gridirons every Saturday before crowds that attest the wholesome public interest in vigorous young American manhood. Thus, it may fairly be said that fraternities are responsible for the two main activities that make college worth while—their own activities and athletics. Without fraternities we should, of course, lack the first, and athletics would be on so low a plane that they could not redeem our colleges from their fundamental futility.

But we have yet to mention the most graceful and distinctive contribution of the college fraternities—their quaint and charming songs. All fraternities devote much time to choral singing. At the dinner table they sing before dinner, between courses, after dinner; indeed, at any time they are likely to break into song with a joyous, exuberant spontaneity which proves that American youth—at any rate the better class of American youth—has a deep appreciation of the finer things of life. Whenever one member starts a song, everyone must join, regardless of his preoccupation at the moment—it is one of the unalterable rules of fraternity life. The members may not know the tune of their fraternity song from the Internationale, they may be conversing with the most distinguished guests, they may have their mouths full of hot potato, yet sing they must when the first note is sounded. Occasionally fastidious guests are annoyed and offended at being sprayed with half-masticated food at the inopportune starting of a song, but there seems to be no way to avoid such inconvenience without destroying the spontaneity of the singing.

Fraternity songs are self-congratulatory, it is true; but so are the great patriotic songs of all nations and peoples. The Germans sing *Deutschland Uber Alles,* the Americans sing of their own *Star Spangled Banner,* the British sing of their own King. In a favorite Beta Theta Pi fraternity song there is a definite statement that only Betas go to Heaven when they die, which is certainly an exaggeration but, no doubt, largely harmless. In the songs of each of the fraternities, that particular fraternity is invariably called "best fraternitie"; yet this could not possibly be true. Only a superficial knowledge of statistics is needed to see that only one fraternity could be best in general. Each might be best in some particular respect, to be sure. It might excel in wealth or dress or manners, in the abundance or quality of its liquor or in its capacity to drink the same; but only one fraternity could really be best in a broad sense. Perhaps these organizations should not be censured for their claims, however, because it would be awkward, unmusical, and perhaps even humiliating for a fraternity to sing of its being the "next-best" fraternity or the "third-best" or the "tenth-best" or the "next-worst," even if it were possible to find the exact relative standing of the various groups. All things considered, the matter is best as it is. It is to the credit of the fraternities that they often sing the songs of other fraternities—those in the same grade. Fraternity songs are destined to be America's imperishable folk songs.

Fraternity choral singing is by no means perfect in detail, to be sure; and it may be hoped that it will improve in certain respects. Some members have voices trained mostly in calling the cattle home; others sometimes show an individualistic tendency to sing in a different key from that selected by the leader or perhaps in a variety of keys successively or in no definite key at all—perhaps influenced by the analogy of no-par stock in corporate financing. Often the leader starts the songs too high, forcing the basses into falsetto, or too low, throwing the entire burden on the basses. Even more unfortunate it is that the fraternity membership does not ordinarily provide a harmonious balance of voices. The voices are always predominantly baritone, and it is not uncommon to hear as many as forty baritones singing a cyclonic lead with only a voice or two holding a tenuous barber-shop tenor and as many providing an inadequate bovine substructure of bass. It is to be regretted that God, in his infinite wisdom and mercy, did not create more and better tenors and basses or that the fraternities do not choose their members with more consideration for their voices for they need more tenors and basses. It is to be hoped that they will give their earnest attention to this matter.

The cultural advantages of fraternity life go far beyond the singing of folk songs. In many institutions the pledges are required to learn the Greek alphabet and are thus able not only to distinguish their respective houses generally but to apprehend much of the spirit of Greek life and literature. For students in law, pharmacy and engineering whose work includes little that is cultural, the fraternity thus provides all the cultural advantages that are available.

Fraternity singing is only one of the manifestations of that fine spirit of brotherhood which is the final great contribution of fraternities to American college life. Utopian dreamers have never pictured anything finer than this—this picture of young men living together, sharing each other's shirts and ties and shoes and experiences, breaking bread together, drinking from the same keg. Many a young man, perhaps an only child reared at home alone with mother and father, has found himself at college in a family compared with which that of Brigham Young or the Jukes or Kallikaks seems race suicide indeed—a family of fifty or sixty brothers or, including the chapters in other institutions, literally thousands of brothers. All those in the house he, of course, knows intimately; and he can keep in touch with brothers in other institutions by reading the fraternity quarterly, a very interesting publication which keeps up-to-date records of all the chapter members everywhere. Loyal fraternity men devote much of their time to reading this quarterly, which contains not only the family record but much other valuable information as well. A few news items from this quarterly show clearly the wide range of interests covered:

From Alpha of Arizona: "Brother Lucky Lumpson ranked fourth in the intramural ping-pong tournament this fall. Lucky lags in nothing but grade points."

From Delta of North Dakota: "Brother Zip Zipperson was elected to the student council last week. Zip zips forward irresistibly."

From Iota of Iowa: "Sister Hetty Hogan has been elected to the Y.W.C.A. board. Iota chapter has morals to burn."

From Kappa of Kansas: "Kappa chapter has made her November payment on the house mortgage. Only ninety-nine more payments to make! Plans are being drawn for a new house."

From Chi of Colorado: "Grand Secretary Major Commission was with us to help in the initiation of ten new men. The initiation fees paid in amounted to $150, of which $2.69 goes to our local treasury as the nucleus of a fund for the relief of imbecile children."

It is a fine tribute to the vitality of the fraternity spirit that here in a world of selfishness, a world dominated by the acquisitive ideal, a world governed by the savage warfare of economic competition we should be able to preserve this oasis of Christian brotherhood. It seems like a bit of the Quaker church transplanted to every college campus. Here in the fraternities the young men and women have a comforting sense of initiation, of inclusion, of belonging, a sense of unity, of homogeneity; here they are sheltered from the responsibility of individual differentiation with all its stresses and strains, from the hard necessity of making individual choices and decisions. Here they are happy, much as those newly converted to the Christian faith are happy—in fact, they appear to be even happier because they are saved here and now in the very real present, in the tangible flesh and at an age when they can enjoy being saved.

"Brother," "sister," what depths of selective and discriminating love these words bring to mind—selective and discriminating, yet broadly and generously encompassing a mighty family circle that reaches every part of the land. "Brother," "sister"—these are the words that bring to mind all those intellectual and spiritual ties that bind similar souls and homogeneous hearts together, the magic words that synchronize the heartbeats of those attuned to like ideals, the call from the deep of one human spirit to another across the desert of human selfishness, indifference and preoccupation, the echo from soul to soul of the unvoiced aspirations of fraternal love and kinship. The world grows maudlin over the love of mother for child; yet this is but a biological instinct, common to all mammals, no different in essence from the love of the cow for her calf, the frog for her tadpole, utterly undiscriminating and unselective. The mother must take her children "mine run"; blood brothers and sisters must accept blood brothers and sisters as God sends them— and a motley assortment they may well be, with no common denominator of spiritual attributes. In the fraternities, on the other hand, we find no low affinity of consanguineous biological affiliates but the mutual and reciprocal love of noble spirits chosen for their homogeneous nobility.

And fraternity life is also preparation for the finer things in the world into which the students must soon enter—preparation for the orders of Elks and Moose and other herbivora, for Lions and Rotary and Kiwanis, for all the brotherly orders that hold hands and sing together. Students who have sung their songs together in their chapter houses are well trained in voice and spirit to sing that great classic of American brotherhood, *The More We Get Together the Happier We'll Be*. After four years of convivial bibbing, these friendly spirits are ready for the Elks and the athletic clubs and other festive orders; after several years of whooping 'er up for the best fraternity, men are psychologically and vocally adjusted to the great task of boosting the home town or the home state or the American home in general. They do not become crabbed critics, cynics, knockers, misanthropes or misery-mongers. They are not introverts. They have the peppy zeal, the helpful, cooperative spirit that has made America what it is—or whatever it is. Fraternity members receive the best possible training for constructive citizenship, and their membership should carry college credit. Professors and academicians will object to this, of course; but it is time that we cease to magnify our little world of stale lectures and laboriously compiled books and face the realities of the great busy world. It is time for the colleges to face squarely the problem of training their students for life.

Although my thesis is the defense of fraternities, I hope I may be pardoned if I offer a single hint of criticism, or perhaps it should be termed a friendly warning. Few have dared to point out, indeed apparently few have even noticed, that here in these swanky academic palaces is to be found what may prove to be one of the most insidious forces working toward the destruction of American political institutions. With all their patient and pertinacious vigilance, none of the investigating committees engaged in ferreting out subversive influences in our colleges have observed that in these fraternities we have probably the most sinister threat of communism to be found anywhere in our land. Here indeed *is* communism in actual operation, for these men or women, within the walls of their splendid houses, have abolished most property rights and have built up what is, in its internal organization, a Marxian classless society. The fraternity brothers and sisters own their houses in common, their furniture, rugs and other household equipment; they pay dues equally for maintenance and living expenses and parties; they eat the same food at the same tables with the same service; members who have cars or cigarettes are expected to share them with the brotherhood. With the exception of the cellar gangs already referred to, no class distinctions are drawn. It is true that each member buys his own clothes and toothbrushes or permits his parents to buy them for him; and there is some variation in the quality of clothes worn; but most things are used communistically. Those who graduate are even expected to help buy new houses for future brothers, for all fraternities are either buying new houses or trying to pay for those they have already bought. When a house has been paid for, it is always too small and too shabby.

This gilded and tinselled communism is a far greater danger than the shabby radicalism of the academic proletarians for it commands the respect, admiration and envy of students and of the outside world. The parents of these well-bred young communists are not riff-raff. They are men and women of wealth, prestige and power; and it is difficult to see how they can long escape the infection of the Marxian spirit that pervades the fraternity barracks. Their children bring it home to them, and they even visit their children at school. The danger is all the more insidious because neither parents nor children recognize it; both find the greatest happiness in a way of life which, if it were to spread and permeate American domestic, economic and political life, would mean the destruction of those institutions which most of us hold sacred. I mention this only from a relentless sense of public duty. I am loath to cast a cloud over so much innocent happiness, particularly since there is always a possibility that the danger may not be very great, a possibility that fraternity communism may not spread very far. Yet we may well remember that eternal vigilance is the price of maintaining our sacred traditions.

*Children probably do more harm than dogs. . .*

# FIT TO BE TIED

*A letter written to the editor of the Lawrence Daily
Journal-World when the city council passed an ordinance requiring dogs in Lawrence to be tied up during
the summer months.*

Editor
Lawrence Daily Journal-World

It is cheering to know that the city council is going
to save our gardens from the dogs—cheering to everybody but the dogs and the people who like to see dogs
happy. If the dogs have an unhappy summer, they can
console themselves with the thought that they are helping to win the war, that their loss is our eternal gain; or
if they entertain themselves barking at the sun and
moon, that will add zest to our lives in another way.
In any case, the pups can look forward to the cold days
next winter when they will be free to roam about in
the gardens. Dogs live too much in the present, anyhow, and should be encouraged to look forward more.

But the council should expand the coverage of this
protective legislation. Children probably do more harm
than dogs and should be tied up in the back yard with
the dogs; and a considerable number of grownups

would be better off tied to the porch post than roaming around freely, especially at night. They don't trample the gardens, but some of them do worse. Perhaps it would be well to tie the city council up with the children and the dogs so that the councilmen could observe the practical operation of this legislation and so that they would not pass any more like it. Dogs running loose are bad enough; but a city council running loose, that's pretty bad, too. It is fortunate that our councilmen are kind and humane men. After all, they did not poison our dogs!

It is true this dog ordinance has deprived us of an important uplifting influence. A dozen dogs playing happily and peaceably on the campus, with scarcely a dog fight once a year, were an inspiring sight to those of us who had been reading about the conduct of peoples, of nations of human beings. Seeing these dogs at play, we were inspired to work and strive ceaselessly to raise mankind to the level of assorted mongrel dogs. It was a high ideal, a noble purpose, unattainable of course, yet worthy of our striving. It is doubtful if a thousand bored and lonely dogs yelping at their ropes will provide an equal amount of equally high inspiration.

—John Ise

# CONSUMERS' VALUES IN A CRAZY WORLD

*An address delivered before the Midwest Economics Association, really written long ago for relaxation.*

Something over two thousand years ago, a very strange people lived in Southeastern Europe on the shores of the Mediterranean Sea. Poverty-stricken, these people lived in houses without drains and without stoves, slept in beds without sheets or springs, fastened their clothes without buttons, wore no underclothes and no socks, warmed themselves over a pot of ashes, "studied poetry without books, geography without maps and politics without newspapers"; and they had no gadgets. Yet, in their rags and hovels they produced some of the greatest literature, philosophy, painting and sculpture of all ages. Never knowing comfort, the Greeks built what was in some respects the highest civilization ever known.

Nearly two thousand years later another race of barbarians, also without furnaces or automobiles or gadgets, began to write music. The great German musicians, Bach, Mozart, Beethoven and Schubert, never housed comfortably, never able to travel at 60 miles an hour, without any of the advantages of rapid transit, Chambers of Commerce, Liberty Leagues, Daughters of the First American Revolution, red networks, moving pictures, daily tabloids or funnies or football carnivals, turned their attention to the writing of immortal music.

A century or two later, a great and highly civilized people, mostly descendants of the fifty thousand heroes who braved the dangers of the briny deep in the good ship Mayflower in order to give the pagan Indians the blessings of rum and Christian civilization, found a new way of life which was to be the efflorescence of many centuries of developing culture.

They bought books that they had no time to read, pianos they could not play, victrolas and records they should not have played, pictures they could not understand; they built houses that they did not want to live in—with recreation rooms where they had no time to recreate. They invented engines and thermostats, statistics and scientific management, advertising and salesmanship, B.O. and halitosis, dental cripples and dishpan hands, cathedral bathrooms, calories and vitamins, cigar lighters and near beer, crooning, kidnapping and school girl complexions; but, alas, they knew not Plato, and they knew not Beethoven. Their unquenchable energies they devoted to the perfection of new engines with which to transport themselves quickly from places where they were bored to tears to other places where they were bored to death. Knowing the substantial joy of being comfortable, they worked themselves into hardened arteries and high blood pressure and Bright's disease devising new ways of being still more comfortable until they attained a level of bodily comfort quite as high as that of hogs in the shade of the old apple tree. Indifferent to the pain and tedium that they suffered in leisure time, they invented numberless gadgets to provide still more leisure time which they devoted to such cultural activities as bridge, fan dancing, brotherly lodges and ballyhoo, cross-word puzzles, flagpole sitting, stamp collecting, walkathons, endurance flying, and organizations for the uplift of the underprivileged classes that have no leisure time in which to be bored. They applied their talents to the invention of new gewgaws with which to protect themselves from the boredom of their own intellectual and cultural aridity, to the task of learning to use the gadgets that they had in their cars and kitchens and bathrooms and to the protection of American gadget civilization from insidious communists. They were so busy with all these manifold activities that they had little time for the study of any form of art, which was thought unmanly anyhow and unworthy of a great nation of rugged individualists. The study of the arts was left to the women, who had been released from domestic duties by the gadgets in the homes.

The culture of these people was in great measure due to the habit of associating much with each other for the mutual sharing of ideas, like orangoutangs, oysters and termites. They had clubs for all functions: for playing bridge and cooking and singing and reading and dancing and hunting and fishing and traveling and gardening and eating and drinking and worshipping—clubs in which rich men hired athletes to take exercise for them, clubs for the protection of American democracy from alien radicals or from the Democrats or from the Republicans or from too much democracy.

Perhaps all this will seem like a criticism of what

is often called American civilization; but before we can offer a criticism of that hypothetical abstraction, we must analyze it in the light of cold and scientific logic. Can we say that devotion to gadgets is inferior to the study of Plato or Beethoven? Can we say, categorically, that the pleasure of riding from nowhere to nowhere at 80 miles an hour is inferior in quality to the pleasure of listening to the *Eroica Symphony* or the *Götterdämmerung*? As economists, we have always evaded such questions. We have assumed that whatever the people want has economic utility whether bootleg gin or Beethoven, and from the predominance of demand for the former have assumed that American happiness was increasing day by day in every way. Economists have refused to make distinctions among different satisfactions because they thought themselves unfitted to the task and unable to make any worthwhile contribution. I share the modesty of all economists in this matter, but the importance of the problem will perhaps justify even a feeble effort at its elucidation.

Perhaps much of our traditional economics is pointless and of little avail, a foundation with no superstructure, a prologue without the opera. The production of goods, more goods, more things, mountains of things— to what purpose? The assumption is that more goods mean more satisfactions, more utility, more comfort and happiness. The assumption seems to be that man has an infinite capacity for pleasurable titillations and that titillations of all kinds are equally good for him. The truth appears to be that men are so constituted as to be capable of only a limited number of titillations, that above a pain economy the goods to which men are accustomed fade into the background and cease to have psychological importance. Only the new, unusual or unaccustomed goods stir any conscious response. The bicycle of a generation ago brought as much satisfaction as the automobile of today. The increased health and cleanliness of our age of wealth represent objective gains; but in other respects, it is doubtful if our mountains of goods have made us any happier than the poverty-stricken pioneers of a generation or two ago. Increase in human happiness and, much more certainly, improvement in the *quality* of life must be found in something else.

Consumers' goods may be classified in a great many ways; but, following Professor Hawtrey, I shall begin by dividing them into *defensive* goods, those which serve merely to prevent pain or distress, and *creative* goods, those which supply some positive, creative satisfaction. Food enables us to avoid hunger; clothing with our furnaces and thermostats, enables us to avoid cold; knee action cars enable us to avoid being jolted, although we may sometimes pay $5 a day for a riding horse to give us the jolts we miss in the car; by riding to the golf club in a car we may avoid the fatigue of walking so that we may enjoy the fatigue of playing golf; the electric eye shifts our gears and opens the door and turns the water fountain on for us, relieving us of exhausting and fatiguing labor so that we may take our morning setting-up exercises with more zest. Jazz, most novels, most movies, cards and puzzles and dice enable us to avoid boredom— which we may define as "an uncomfortable consciousness of cerebral innocuous desuetude." All the goods and products I have mentioned are merely defensive, as are most of the goods that litter the rooms of our homes and the shelves of our stores. They enable us to avoid hunger, cold, discomfort, fatigue, pain or boredom. They are merely negative.

Perhaps we should ask how far is distress bad. We are safe in saying that unallayed hunger, cold and fatigue, characteristic of a pain economy, are bad because they are destructive of health or even of life—which for the present I shall assume to be good. Yet, without hunger there could be no joy of eating; without cold, warmth could scarcely be felt as a good; without fatigue there could be no sweet rest. It is good to be hungry if we presently may eat, to be cold if we may warm ourselves, to be tired if we soon may rest. The want is inseparable from the satisfaction of it. One of the faults of our age of plenty is that we seldom feel keen hunger, physical fatigue or cold and, therefore, miss in part the substantial satisfactions of a simpler and more meager economy. Pain is bad, however, because it is symptomatic of a danger to health or life; boredom is similarly bad, indicating a lack of vigorous intellectual health. The distress that arises from dirt is bad because of its obvious relation to health, although cleanliness is sometimes carried beyond the needs of health to proclaim a "pecuniary capacity for conspicuous consumption," particularly when we may bathe in the cathedral bathrooms of the modern home. At any rate we look forward to Saturday night with far more joy than our pioneer ancestors did.

Many defensive products such as thermostats and gadgets serve merely to protect the individual from physical discomfort; but, as Professor Hawtrey says: "The whole yields no positive good; it merely brings him to the zero point at which he is suffering from no avoidable harm."—the point that the aforesaid hogs reached with almost no trouble at all. "The man has weeded his garden and still has to choose what he will plant in it before he can be said to have made anything of his life."

Other defensive products—machines and gadgets—increase the amount of leisure, but to no worthwhile end. The oyster and the crab have leisure, likewise the heiress and the playboy at Miami; but they build no noble lives. What does the typical man do with his leisure? "To create leisure," as Hawtrey says, "and then to occupy it by killing time is a contemptible confession of failure"; yet, that is precisely what this man does. The most effective and conclusive way to kill time is, of course, to commit suicide. That disposes of a great amount of leisure time and eliminates all boredom at once; but few have the courage to follow this logical course. Temporary suicide and release from boredom may be achieved by getting drunk. A considerable number avail themselves of this escape. Analogous to this is the playing of certain games—bridge and poker—which enable men and women to tide over tedious afternoons or nights without undue mental strain. Many men and women resort to cards. Automobile riding is for many a defense against boredom, which accounts for the great popularity of the automobile. To sit and think involves mental strain; to merely sit is tedious; but to sit and drive is neither straining nor tedious; and the car radio turned to Happy Hooligan's horrible jazz adds nothing to the demands on the mind. Most movies, newspapers—particularly the funny sections—most popular magazines such as the *American* and *True Confessions*, most of the music heard over the radio serve merely to protect people from being bored.

Here we can make out the fundamental reason for

the multiplicity of organizations, societies and clubs in America and for the overpowering anxiety of most people to join as many as possible. I know a town of 150 inhabitants which has 151 organizations of various kinds. I agree with Schopenhauer that it is better to be alone than with a hundred fools, but it is probably better for any one of the fools to be with the other ninety-nine. It is so much more sociable, and there is less danger of being bored.

Creative goods are goods which serve in building a richer and finer life—a life definitely above that of the hogs in the shade of the old apple tree. The hogs are not hungry; they do not suffer from cold or heat; they are comfortable, unfatigued and contented. The creative life must be something above this; and good music, good literature, artistic creations of all kinds are competent to raise life above this physical and biological level.

A second distinction among different kinds of goods and activities we need not discuss here—the distinction based on social consequences. America stands today in very great danger of lapsing back to some form of barbarism because too many people are playing bridge and studying gadgets who should be reading and discussing economics, sociology and political science. Perhaps the development of a taste for good music and the fine arts would not help much here; but good literature broadens the social outlook, perhaps quite as much as technical economics and so is real training in intelligent citizenship.

A very important distinction and one which the economist can use safely is that based on the question of durability. A good sort of satisfaction, like a good coat, is one which lasts well, while a poor one, like a shoddy garment, soon wears thin. Here is a clear and objective distinction, one that does not lead us into the brambles of aesthetics.

By adopting this distinction, we avoid the pitfalls always involved in contrasting high and low wants. Many people speak of certain satisfactions as low—eating and drinking, for instance and of others as high—the enjoyment of literature, music and the other fine arts. The distinction is not clear and exact, however, for any of the satisfactions mentioned may be either high or low; and it may take generations to find out which. The real question is, *does it wear well?* If the dedication of much time and attention to the niceties of eating brings lasting happiness, it is good; if it finally palls or if it brings gout or overweight or indigestion, it is bad. If indulgence in Bach or Beethoven proves to be a lasting and growing source of happiness, we must call it good; if it brings us to satiety and boredom, we must call it bad.

This distinction will serve not only as between different kinds of satisfaction but as between different grades of the same satisfaction. Good furniture is furniture that wears well, not physically but aesthetically; bad furniture seems uglier every time we look at it. We know that Chippendale and Sheraton models are good because they have stood the test of many generations. Good literature is literature that wears well; poor literature is that of which we tire quickly, that which is soon forgotten. Let anyone read Artemus Ward or Bill Nye a few times and note the rate at which the utility declines; then, let him read Mark Twain a few times. It is easy to pick out the great literature. Mark Twain, like Walt Whitman, once regarded as vulgar, is now recognized as one of the greatest writers of all time.

Like a garment of fine cloth, a service of sterling silver, a statue hewn by Praxiteles, he *wears well.*

The same principle applies to music and painting and all the fine arts. I recall a time when I could read a world of symphonic drama into the Spanish fandango, when a Dudley Buck love song made me want to marry all the girls in the Sears Roebuck catalogue. Most of us go through such a period of immaturity. Most of us test out the various grades and qualities of music and, if we have any capacity for growth, wind up with a solid appreciation of the great masters. Good music *wears well.* I confess that I have some difficulty with Bach—perhaps because I still enjoy romance in music and because, when I hear his fugues, I can just see his 20 children chasing each other around the table.

To make a further confession, I do not enjoy most modern music; and I find it difficult to apply my criterion of durability. I never did like the stuff and it sounds no worse the second time than the first—and usually no better. Since I cannot test it myself, I shall have to leave the task of its appraisal to my grandchildren. Much of it sounds the way mid-Victorian furniture looks, and I doubt if most of it will stand the test of time; but another generation will be able to speak authoritatively.

This brings me to a final criterion for judging human recreational activities and satisfactions. What do they do to us? Do they cause us to shrink and shrivel and harden like the meat of a stale walnut; or do they help us to grow into a broader, deeper and richer appreciation of the fine things in life? Alfred Marshall says that the fullness of life is found in the development of as *many* and as *high* faculties as possible.

Mind, I do not speak of *happiness.* I do not know

what happiness is. Some philosophers say there is no such thing; others say that it is merely a matter of individual judgment. I find it is not a by-product of education; and I think education should not have the purpose of making people happy. "Its aim," as Frank Knight says, "is rather to raise problems than to solve them: the association of sadness and wisdom is proverbial, and he that increaseth knowledge increaseth sorrow." Most of my idiot friends, on the other hand, seem contented with the world as it is, happy in spite of all the world-wide grief and distress that make philosophers sad. Pictures of complete happiness: a million Germans, a few years ago, with their brains turned off, yelling "Heil Hitler"; 25,000 students throwing their hats in the air when the home team makes a touchdown; 100,000 patriotic Americans at a political convention or rally, with bands and ballyhoo saving America from God knows what! No, education does not aim to make people happy, nor does culture, nor civilization itself.

If we define happiness as comfort and satiety and contentment, we may even go further and say that happiness is not always what men seek. As Frank Knight suggests, run through a list of economic wants, food, clothing, shelter, amusement, etc., and "ask the candid question as to what fraction of the ordinary man's expenditure for any of them makes him feel better, or is expected to do so." "It is a stock and conclusive objection to utopias," to quote Knight again, "that men simply will not live in a world where everything runs smoothly and life is free from care . . . . A man who has nothing to worry about immediately busies himself in creating something, gets into some absorbing game, falls in love, prepares to conquer some enemy, or hunt lions or the

North Pole, or what not. We recall also the case of Faust, that the Devil himself could not invent escapades and adventures fast enough to give his soul one moment's peace. So he died, seeking and striving; and the Angel pronounced him thereby 'saved.' *Wer immer strebend sich bemüht, den können wir erlösen* . . . . The pleasure philosophy is a false theory of life. The Hindus thought the question of happiness through to the end long ago and reached the inevitable conclusion—*Nirvana*—just life enough to enjoy being dead."

Here we part with those whom Carlyle calls the "pig-trough philosophers." The fullness of life is not found in the consumption of the most possible goods, in the eating of the most delicately flavored food, the wearing of the richest garments, the living in many-roomed houses. That direction lies not life but satiety and envy and boredom.

No, I am not talking about happiness which I can't define and if I could define, wouldn't want badly enough to dispense with what brains I have in order to get it. I am talking about *life, the fullness of life*—the exercise of as many and as high faculties as possible. I do not know whether life is good or not; but if it isn't good, we can help ourselves liberally, anyhow, while we are here and console ourselves with the thought that we can be dead a long while. Since I must have such a large helping of being dead, I would like to be as much alive as possible while I am here. I would like to exercise as many and as high faculties as possible. I want to live with my family, I want to read much, listen to the riches of music, travel, see the beauties of nature and great works of art, see a good show occasionally, fish a little when I have the patience, perhaps play golf, hunt antiques, dig in the ground in the springtime—I believe it was Abel who started that business, and man will never get away from it—walk through dead leaves in November, and through snow in the winter. As a good Kansas man, reared in the rarified moral atmosphere of Kansas, I cannot, of course, indulge in strong drink even for the stomach's sake; but I can enjoy 3.2 beer on hot summer days and a cigar when I have a dime. We need not get full to have a full life, but I suppose a full life would have to include a moderate amount of wickedness.

The exercise of "as many and as high faculties as possible"—that is the good life because it is *much* life. It is on this principle that man, or at any rate *some* men, may be said to be higher than the oyster. Having a somewhat larger and more deeply convoluted brain, a man *may* indeed be wiser than an oyster; but he may also be *crazier* than an oyster. Having greater resources, he can know so much more that isn't so. An investigation of political intelligence by Professor Eldridge of the University of Kansas revealed the fact that on some economic questions, men knew much less than nothing—that on some true-false questions they batted only 25 per cent. Any colony of oysters could bat 50 per cent, as could tin men or weather vanes—on the mathematical principle of probability. Man is not necessarily wiser than an oyster; but according to Marshall, he lives a fuller life because he exercises more faculties. Some philosophers express somewhat the same ideal in what they call the "development of personality."

Using this criterion, how shall we appraise some of the current recreational activities? Is the professional society woman a wiser, finer, nobler character because of her expensive parties? Is she learning to live more fully—"to exercise more or higher faculties"? Does the devotee of bridge grow steadily in high faculties from wondering who played the jack or who holds the ace? Man, made in the image of God, cudgeling his brains about such a question—it is blasphemy! Surely such a question is hardly worthy even of a woman—made of an ancestral rib. Does the baseball fan develop new richness of personality by listening to the radio announcer describe the game someone else is playing? Is the movie fan typically a man of many high faculties because of his devotion to such noble dramas as *French Line* and *Naughty Marietta*? No, these activities are merely defensive. They are resorted to by those who are trying to protect themselves from boredom. Even in our colleges, we find the students engaged mainly in activities of this sort. Nature, as the physicists say, abhors a vacuum; and some of our students would be almost complete vacua were it not for social and athletic activities.

What, by the way, do these activities do to our typical student? They leave him stranded in early middle life, a cultural wreck—or shall I say a "flat tire" or a cultural doughnut with the rim knocked off—with nothing to carry him on through the rest of his flat, stale and unprofitable journey. "Fat and forty," he can no longer dance; his favorite magazines, the *American* and *Ballyhoo*, no longer satisfy even with the lift afforded by his Camels; athletics are hardly safe for his weak heart even when described over the radio; jazz is warmed-over gravy. So he must protect himself from the growing weight of tedium by joining brotherly lodges, dressing himself up in a dunce cap and parading the streets, making speeches on the necessity of preserving the Constitution—which he has never read—and perhaps indulging in a glorious alcoholic release once in a while on the occasion of a visit to his noble *Alma Mater*.

Yet I would not like to seem unappreciative of our students. They are the finest people in the world, the only redemption—if there is any redemption—of our educational system. Their faults are merely the faults of American life, and their virtues rise above the ordinary level of American life. I am quite out of sympathy with the cynic who described American education as "the casting of false pearls before real swine." Some of our pearls are seconds, Woolworth pearls, I think; but our students, God bless them, are as fine as could be reared in a comfort-, gadget-, and speed-worshipping civilization—or shall I say "barbarism"?

Building for a full life—that is what we need—the development of a taste for the *enduring* cultural values, for *good* literature and art and music, the sort of things that pile up spiritual riches within us and leave us wondering not how we shall pass the time but how we can find time for all the beauty that is within our reach.

In a civilization like ours, good music, literature and the arts are needed as never before. Ours is a technological civilization, a civilization of iron and steel, of wheels and cranes and levers, of science and engineering, of roar and clatter. It is a civilization in which realism has displaced romance, in which the emotions have shrivelled in the glare of harsh reality. The man without capacity for emotional experience may be very scientific, but his life is on a dead level of monotony that smacks of spiritual death. We need emotional experience which we can find better in music than anywhere else, in the nobility of Beethoven's *Eroica Symphony*, in the pathos of Tchaikovsky's *Symphony Pathétique*, or Schubert's *Tod und das Maedchen*, in the ecstatic grief of the *Liebestod*. As a release from the hard realities of a machine age, we need good music and the fine arts to keep our souls alive.

One more thought I would like to leave with you. If our economic society is not incurably sick, we may look forward to much more leisure time in the future— leisure time which we may kill by playing cards, reading the tabloids or driving our cars rapidly past our splendid system of billboards, or which we may use to build up our own cultural resources. Unfortunately our business civilization provides excellent facilities for our degradation but not much that is uplifting. The radio, which might afford us riches undreamed of is prostituted to jazz and the advertisement of contented cows, Nutrena chicken feed and Skelly miracle gasoline. Here is the greatest failure of American democracy—in the sense that it falls farther short of its possibilities for good than anything else I can think of. The government should broadcast over the radio at all times during the day and evening on different wave lengths, grand opera, symphony orchestra music, chamber music with intermissions of oratorio, jazz of two grades—plain rotten and infernal— lectures by the greatest speakers in the country and Bob Hope throughout the day. You will see that I am no snob. I want the cultural proletariat to have their ham and eggs. I would gladly give them the largest and worst jazz orchestras that money will buy and Bob Hope on one wave length but not on 20.

This program would call for an expenditure of perhaps a few hundred million dollars a year—one or two cents a day per capita. It would give employment to thousands of competent musicians; and it would make America a decent place to live in, even for those who love good music.

Something tells me, however, that all this is not in prospect. Something tells me that if, when, and as we again see peace, we shall have more and worse jazz, bigger and better bridge parties, gadgets piled on gadgets, longer and faster cars and happier fools driving them faster past bigger and better billboards; and I suppose we shall always have pessimists worrying about a possible decline of such civilization.

. . ."Umbrella Uplift Decree". . .

# EXCELSIOR: A STORY OF TARIFF PROSPERITY

*A paper written many years ago in an effort to reduce to absurdity the arguments for tariff protection.*

The great fundamental economic truth that a protective tariff increases imports of goods was first enunciated in the closing years of the reign of the Little Pickle Prosperity President. It was first clearly expressed in his message to Congress in December, 1927.

This epochal message was little understood by contemporaries and was even derided by some of the men of the time, particularly by the academic economic theorists. The principle announced was beyond the grasp, beyond the understanding of the great, thoughtless multitude; and it seems even possible that it might have passed into history, might have been buried in the bulky tomes of the Congressional Record like the petition of the City of Baal for a new post office, had not another prophet of the same school brought it forward a second time—the great Efficiency Engineer Economist, Herbert Hercules, who was candidate for the high office of president.

The specific point thus wet-nursed by the great Efficiency Engineer was that a tariff is an *unmixed* blessing, that it does not even have the effect of reducing imports of goods. On the contrary, strange as it may seem to those uninitiated into the mysteries of economic legerdemain, the higher the tariff on imports—the more imports are shut out—the more prosperous the people become; the more they are able to pay for imports; and the more imports are brought into the country.

There was much debate of the matter. Theoreticians said that if foreign goods were kept out of the country less foreign goods would be imported. They declared that this was an elementary proposition which even the lowest class of Republicans ought to be able to understand; but they were mistaken in this as the election proved. Indeed, it appeared that even many Democrats could not understand it perfectly.

When the election was over, all classes clamored for their respective shares of the general blessings of protection. Of course, the iron and steel and woolen and lumber and cotton and sugar manufacturers were treated generously as was proper. The laborers were given protection against cheap food and clothing and against books and pictures made by the pauper laborers of other countries and against the cheap sugar which is so often the cause of diabetes. Then the farmers were protected from cheap lumber, cheap woolen and cotton clothing, cheap jack-knives, and, like the laborers, from the diabetic cheap sugar. Thus was the health of the common people preserved and their morals also protected from the disintegration that always follows contact with cheap goods. Some of the farmers did not like to pay high prices for their goods just to preserve their morals, but it was pointed out to them that no lasting prosperity could come to the farmers anyhow unless it went to the great manufacturers first and from them percolated out to the farmers.

This great principle was very difficult for some of the more ignorant farmers to grasp. Some of them even argued that the best way to make them prosperous would be to give them more for what they had to sell and not to charge them more for what they had to buy; but this was of course only the short view of the matter and was soon seen to be such. Some of the agricultural statesmen, with clearer and broader vision than the rest, even urged that the agricultural states appropriate money to send to the big manufacturers to make them more prosperous so they could buy more of the farmers' products. Church collections were often sent in the same way; and in some of the more progressive agricultural states, the legislatures passed laws raising the prices of manufactured goods in order that the manufacturers' prosperity might be enhanced.

In all these various ways, many millions of dollars were raised by the farmers and sent to the big manufacturers; and the result was such a wave of prosperity as agriculture had not seen since the time of William McKinley. As the far-seeing protectionist statesmen had anticipated, the more the farmers sent to the great manufacturers, the more prosperous, of course, were the manufacturers; the more laborers they were able to hire; the higher were the wages at which they were able to hire them; the more pork and beef and eggs and carrots and turnips and rutabagas the manufacturers and the laborers were able to buy from the farmers, the higher the prices they were able to pay and the more prosperous were the farmers; and, of course, the more money they were able to raise to send to the manufacturers again. Thus a beneficent circle of cause and effect was set up which brought great prosperity to all—so great, indeed, that if it had not been for the zealous care with which the protectionist statesmen guarded the morals of the people, many of the common people might have suffered from this prosperity. Common people are very easily debauched.

But the farmers wanted protection on their farm products too. The wheat producers asked for enough protection to make them so prosperous that they could import various luxuries from Europe and South America; and appropriate duties were levied on all kinds of farm products, with the exception that for some reason there was no tariff on goats. This omission provoked a great deal of discussion. The Democrats said the farmers were the goats. To compensate for the lack of a tariff on goats, a very high duty was levied on camels' hair brushes to encourage the production of camels on the arid plains of the West. It was pointed out that camels had picturesque and exotic virtues which goats lacked. This wise provision very soon brought great prosperity to some of the hitherto unproductive regions of the United States.

There was some captious criticism of this on the ground that the camels were of no value anyhow since no one wanted to ride camels where there were plenty of automobiles. But this carping criticism was silenced by the Little Pickle Prosperity ex-President himself who, in a statesmanlike message to the newspapers, pointed out that it was the business of consumption to take care of itself. If no one wanted the camels it was not the fault of the government or of the capitalistic system, that the industry had been created, that the money—or at any rate, the camels—were circulating, that it was infinitely better that there should be camels on the arid plains than nothing at all—better that the camels should be here than in Mesopotamia—and that if no one wanted the camels it was the fault of the people and not of the system. This seemed such obviously good economic reasoning that the criticism was silenced, and the Little Pickle Prosperity ex-President was allowed to go back to his fishing to which he had accustomed himself while engaged in the arduous duties of the presidency. The Little Pickle Prosperity President had established the tradition that a president must devote a great deal of time to fishing, which has since been followed by all successful presidents.

During the time when the Great Engineer Economist was raising the tariff, he was also building a great canal along the St. Lawrence River to facilitate foreign trade with Europe; and there were some cantankerous critics, mostly Democrats and theoretical economists, who asserted that there was an inconsistency here, that there was no sense in spending a billion dollars for a canal to reduce the costs of foreign trade while imposing a tariff to raise the expenses of foreign trade, no sense in promoting and at the same time obstructing foreign trade, no sense in spending a billion dollars for a canal to reduce cost when a reduction of the tariff would secure the same results at no cost at all. The Great Engineer Economist, however, pointed out that in the long run the effect of tariffs always was to increase the amount of foreign trade. Therefore, the canal and the tariff would both operate to the same beneficial end—

increasing wealth and prosperity for the people. The canal would be necessary to accommodate the trade which would develop as a result of the tariff; and furthermore, a reduction of the tariff would give no employment whatever, whereas, the digging of the canal would not only give employment and raise wages but would make possible further raising of the tariff, and thus, lay the foundation for even more prosperity.

There was much debate and discussion of the principles involved, not only in Congress, in the President's Cabinet and among the great bankers but among the common people as well, some asserting that the new canal would be a great blessing and others contending that it was an obstacle to the successful operation of the tariff. The Great Engineer Economist finally appointed a commission, the "Water Canal, Boat Shipping and Tariff Enrichment Investigation Commission," to consider the matter. The Commission called in many eminent businessmen and statisticians for consultation and presently issued a report showing that the canal had reduced the cost of shipping wheat eight and three-tenths cents per bushel, that it was therefore encouraging international trade and impeding the enrichment of the people. The Commission recommended an increase of eight and three-tenths cents a bushel in the tariff on wheat as the only logical way to overcome the handicap the canal had imposed.

The tariff was immediately raised as suggested; but while it brought great benefits, it was not as effective as had been hoped because the tariff was on the wrong side of the fence, so to speak. The wheat was moving out of the country and was therefore not subject to the tariff. The farmers were not getting its benefits at all except indirectly through the general enrichment which a tariff always brings to the people. The problem as to how to make the tariff more directly beneficial to the farmers puzzled the greatest minds in the protectionist party; but the Great Engineer Economist finally solved it by sending a commission to Europe to ask the European nations to raise *their* tariffs on wheat. This they were glad to do since the United States had already set the precedent in international amity by raising her tariff on all European goods; and the result was a very great increase in the prosperity of all European countries so that they could buy far more wheat than ever before. In this way farmers received direct benefit from the wheat tariff, the European peoples had more bread to eat, and great prosperity and happiness were enjoyed by all. The League of Nations finally issued an edict requiring all nations to raise their tariffs, and in this way the entire world received the benefits of protection and prosperity.

But the Great Engineer Economist and his protectionist party were not yet content with the blessings that the canal and the tariff had brought to the people. They saw that while the tariff had counteracted the evil effects of the canal, it had not provided the maximum amount of employment for the lower classes; and the Great Engineer Economist issued an edict requiring all vessels using the canal to unload and reload their cargoes at least twice on each trip. This, of course, provided just as much trade obstruction and prosperity as the tariff did; and in addition, it gave employment to labor and raised wages; and since the tariff remained as high as before, the people were doubly blessed. When the Great Engineer Economist saw how much benefit had accrued from canal construction and regulation, he issued still another edict ordering the canal to be filled up and another to be dug. In this way he further increased the amount of employment prosperity.

During the years that all these events were transpiring there was much discussion of the problem of certain war debts that European countries owed the United States for help that the United States had rendered in defeating the wicked, militaristic Kaiser of Germany and for making the world safe for democracy. The European countries claimed that they could not afford to pay their debts so great was the expense involved in preparing for the *next* war to save the world for democracy. There was much agitation in the United States for sending the army to collect the debts just as the United States did with smaller countries; but this plan was finally abandoned because the European armies were already too strong. By a sagacious stroke of diplomacy, the Great Engineer, instead, sent a commission of protectionist statesmen to Europe who persuaded the debtor countries that it would be greatly to their advantage to pay the debts. This commission explained to the European statesmen that the payment of the debts would increase their own prosperity, that if it was beneficial to *keep down* the amount of goods in a country by means of tariffs, it would obviously be much more beneficial to *reduce* the amount of goods in the country by shipping some of them out in payment of debts. As soon as this was explained to the European statesmen they cheerfully agreed to pay and forthwith sent many shiploads of goods to the United States to apply on account.

The result of this was to give much employment in Europe, to raise wages, stimulate enterprise, and increase wealth so rapidly that the European countries could afford better armies than ever before. And, since the support of these armies required the services of many laborers, wages were still further enhanced; and still greater prosperity was enjoyed by the peoples so that they could further increase the size of their armies and also buy more wheat and corn and pork and cotton from the United States.

But while the payment of the debts increased the prosperity of Europe and of the farmers of the United States, it was a very great detriment to the laborers of the United States whom it deprived of needed employment. When Congress raised the tariff, the European countries retaliated by raising their own tariffs, and increased their prosperity so greatly that they could send more goods on account than before. It presented a very serious problem indeed. Finally the Great Engineer Economist sent a commission to Europe to intercede with them to forego the payment of the debt; but they insisted that the debt had been incurred in good faith and they must be allowed to pay it. There was a protection party in European countries too, and they had discovered the secret of tariff prosperity.

There was much perplexity among the statesmen of the United States at this turn of events. They tried to borrow money of Europe so that they might participate in the economic advantage of owing money and paying debts; but the European statesmen would not lend anything although, of course, they had so much money they were hard-pressed to find any way to spend it. Finally, the American statesmen found some very primitive and ignorant people in Africa and Afghanistan from whom they were able to borrow enough money to create a small debt which, to some extent, compensated for the debt the Europeans insisted on paying; and later the President sent spies to Europe who borrowed money secretly and then turned their debts over to the United States government. In this way a very good debt was created which enabled the country to send much goods to Europe and so participate more fully in the general prosperity. Since more and more goods were being sent by all countries—because of their greater prosperity— there was a very great demand for ships, and this gave much employment in the shipyards and further enriched the people everywhere.

When the President saw how the tariffs against European goods had stimulated prosperity and employment and how much benefit followed every increase in the tariff, he reasoned logically that a complete prohibition of imports would be even more beneficial, so he issued a decree to that effect. But the European countries responded with a prohibition of all imports, and for some reason this policy did not prove to be an unmixed blessing. Of course, it gave much employment in Europe just as in the United States; but there was a serious disadvantage involved in it—no country could get rid of its surplus of goods. Wheat and corn and cotton, automobiles, furniture and clothing, goods of all kinds were piled up in the warehouses until the statesmen were greatly troubled as to what to do with them.

There was much agitation about the disposition of surplus goods. Some of the people insisted that there was nothing injurious about goods, that the people could consume them with impunity, that the wheat should be made into bread and eaten, that the clothes should be worn, and that no ill effects would follow. They argued that this was the very purpose for which the goods had been produced. The more farsighted protectionist statesmen explained, however, that the prosperity of every country depended upon exporting a surplus. Otherwise, it could not have a favorable balance of trade and would gradually shrivel and degenerate just as Babylon and Greece and Rome had done.

While the statesmen and the people were debating, the Great Engineer Economist himself called a meeting of the National Commercial Chamber and, with the help of the great business minds, solved the problem in a very simple way by repealing the import prohibition and requiring all foreign vessels to dump their goods in the ocean at least three miles from shore. This happy solution protected American industries and at the same time, enabled the European countries to dispose of their surplus goods. They promptly adopted similar measures, and so the benefit was made general.

There seemed to be no reasonable way of further enriching the people, but the President was indefatigable in his efforts to promote the public interests. He soon issued yet another edict that was the logical sequence of the decrees just recorded. Since dumping goods in the ocean had greatly stimulated industry and trade and employment, it was obvious that sinking the ships would be even more beneficial; so he decreed that the ships should be sunk with the goods. This policy provided a way to get rid of goods and also gave a great stimulus to shipbuilding. Soon the navy yards all over the world were busy; the steel mills were smoking; labor was employed at high wages; and the money circulated to other fields of enterprise, falling like a fertilizing shower over all the world.

There were some people who objected to all this protection against European goods, who insisted that it was no more reasonable to levy tariffs to shut out foreign goods that had already been paid for than it would be for farmers to hold umbrellas over their fields while it was raining, that the tariffs were designed to reduce the amount of goods coming from Europe, and that umbrellas would similarly reduce the goods produced as a result of rains coming from Heaven, that whether the goods came directly from Europe or indirectly from Heaven was immaterial, that protection was no more reasonable in the one case than in the other.

All this was said in a sneering and disrespectful spirit, but the Great Engineer Economist saw clearly the kernel of truth in the suggestion and forthwith issued a decree requiring farmers to hold umbrellas over at least 10 per cent of their crops during every rain. This not only gave a great impetus to umbrella manufacturing, raised wages and furnished employment in that important industry but resulted in a great demand for labor on the farms since every farmer had to keep a large number of laborers against possible sudden showers. Not only were more farm laborers required as a result of the "Umbrella Uplift Decree" but the farmers were able to hire more laborers because their incomes were much greater. Since less corn was raised, prices were higher, more land was required, rents were raised, and the farm owners had much money with which to hire umbrella holders. Thus were wages and profits and rents raised, and employment and enterprise stimulated among the rural people.

So much benefit resulted from the "Umbrella Uplift Decree" that there was strong agitation for an increase in the amount of land protected so it was raised from 10 to 20 per cent. This, of course, increased employment and wages and prosperity still further, so the percentage was raised to 30 per cent; and finally, an edict was issued requiring the farmers to hold umbrellas over all of their crops. For some reason which the greatest minds in the protectionist party have never been able to apprehend fully, this was not a success. At the suggestion of the President, Congress passed a law imposing a 50 per cent tariff on rain and a bounty on cyclones; but this was also unaccountably unsuccessful.

Some people presently advanced the theory that agricultural prosperity could be enhanced as well by importing some sort of destructive bug from Europe, some insect pest which would destroy the crops as by the use of umbrellas and at much less expense. There was much debate about the matter, and a new party was organized known as the "Bug Booster Party" which grew strong enough to win the next election and try out its theory of prosperity. A very destructive pest was found in Madagascar and brought into the country. It proved very efficient, so much so indeed, that it ate all of the crops planted. But to the surprise of the protectionist leaders, this did not bring great prosperity but a period of great unhappiness. Farm prices were high, to be sure, but since the farmers had nothing to sell, they did not receive the full benefit of these high prices. And, of course, the umbrella manufacturing industry suffered greatly; and employment declined, not among the bugs which were very busy but among the umbrella makers and among the umbrella holders on the farms. The situation seemed very serious indeed, and the protectionists were at their wits' end.

Finally the economic experts of the National Commercial Chamber were called in, and after much deliberation they found a solution to the problem. The experts called for the services of an army of entomologists to fight the Booster Bug—thus giving employment to many college graduates and raising wages generally. They were able to reduce the bug destruction to 25 per cent, saving enough crops to give employment again to the umbrella holders. Thus, through the stimulus of bugs and umbrellas and tariffs, the protectionist statesmen were able to raise prosperity and employment to levels never before attained.

By a skillful application of the simple doctrine of protection, the government was soon able to remove practically all the risk from business. Whenever the men engaged in producing any commodity found that they were losing money or that they were making smaller profits than they wished to, they had only to come to the government and ask for more protection. The government guaranteed a fair and reasonable profit—at least to those who had contributed a fair and reasonable amount to the protectionist campaign expenses in the preceding election.

There were some who criticized this policy because it seemed paternalistic, even almost socialistic, and unworthy of the great pluto-anarchists like the Little Pickle Prosperity ex-President and the Efficiency Engineer Economist, both of whom had always stressed the great dangers of government intervention. But it was pointed out that government intervention in the interests of business, particularly in the interest of the fittest class in business, was wholly beneficial, as the great prosperity of the country under protectionist rule had well proved. It

is true that it favored not those who had really failed to
profit, for they were unable to make generous campaign
contributions, but those who had profited greatly and
who were therefore able to contribute heavily, those who
had given most to the campaign expenses. It was easily
made clear to the masses of the people that the business
and government of the country would be far from safe
in the hands of men so devoid of public spirit as to be
unwilling to contribute to election expenses. It was one
of the laws of God, anyhow, that unto those that have
should be given; and the protectionist policy was thus
not only a law of business and of entrepreneurial eugen-
ics but a law of God as well.

There were critics who feared that this policy of
guaranteeing profits to campaign subscribers would
eliminate competition, but that fear was entirely ground-
less for the competition was merely shifted from the field
of manufacturing and buying and selling to the field of
politics. In this way the protectionist policy revived the
waning interest of the people in their political institutions and thus saved our democratic institutions from
atrophy and decay and disintegration.

When it was seen how the obstruction of international trade had increased the wealth and prosperity of
the people, protectionist statesmen began to look about
to see if there were not other kinds of trade that could be
interfered with. Meetings were called where the need
of further interference was explained to the people, and
in Congress there was much debate as to where the interference might begin. Some of the Democrats and Progressives insisted that trade was productive, that it was
part of the economic process by which the people were
fed and clothed and that any reduction in the volume of

domestic trade would certainly reduce the national wealth. But the protectionists argued logically that if the tariff interference with the trade between Canada and the United States could increase the prosperity of the United States—and it was well known that it had increased the wealth of Canada in the same way—a similar interference within the United States would be equally advantageous for all parts of the United States. They pointed out, furthermore, that as the great Efficiency Engineer Economist had so well demonstrated, a tariff does not really reduce trade at all but, in the long run, greatly increases the amount of trade by making the people so much more prosperous. The only real question was as to how many parts the United States could be divided into for the purpose of obstructing trade and enriching the people.

Protectionist statesmen pointed out that it was probably unfortunate that the North had won the Civil War since the country would have grown rich and prosperous much more rapidly if there had been a boundary line between the North and the South where duties could be levied. There was general agreement among the wiser and wealthier people that the first line of division should be between the North and the South along the famous Mason and Dixon line. At the next session of Congress this was accordingly enacted into law to the great joy and felicitation of the people except a few theoretical economists and ignorant Democrats who were more intent on establishing and maintaining their outgrown economic fallacies than they were in providing for the prosperity of the people.

The new Mason and Dixon division gave a tremendous impetus to American enterprise everywhere. The new tariff duties very soon led to phenomenal agricultural development in the North. Cotton and figs and grapefruit and oranges and dates were grown in hothouses in Minnesota and Michigan, and the building of these hothouses provided work for thousands of laborers. It soon appeared that there was no further need for the generous unemployment fund that the Efficiency Engineer Economist President had provided. The heating of these hothouses required so much coal and fuel oil that the coal and oil industries were very soon enjoying great prosperity. When the carpenters and glass workers and coal miners and oil drillers were thus fully employed at high wages, they were able to buy pork and beef and turnips at high prices; and the farmers came in for their share of the general prosperity.

The people of the South, of course, enjoyed similar advantages, for great automobile and shoe factories, packing plants, steel mills, oatmeal factories, and horseradish reducing works were soon built throughout the South. Much employment was given, much money was put in circulation, and great blessings were enjoyed by all. Even some of the Democrats accumulated wealth. And, of course, in the long run the trade between the North and the South was greater than it had ever been before because the people were so much more prosperous.

When it became clear to the people how beneficial was the Mason and Dixon tariff, how those duties enriched all of the people without burdening anyone, some of the states, following the leadership of their commercial chambers, demanded tariffs around their borders to build up the various industries that they lacked.

The commercial chambers advocated this farsighted

policy with the purpose of keeping money at home. It
was at first unconstitutional; but when the necessity for
interstate tariffs was clearly seen, the Constitution was
changed. Each of the states placed heavy duties on all
imports from other states. These duties were soon found
to have the effect of creating vast industries in all of the
states and of enriching the people just as the national
tariff and the Mason and Dixon duties had done. They
also kept much money at home.

The State of Kansas was greatly blessed and enriched by her tariff for Kansas had been an agricultural
state; and when the tariff was raised high enough, it
brought great industries into the state and put much
money in circulation therein. Several steel mills were
built, three in Kansas City, two in Salina, one in El Dora-
do and one in Cawker City. It was at first very difficult
to find iron ore for the new industry, but the rugged individualism and enterprise of the people overcame all
obstacles. They found iron ore in the geological strata
several thousand feet deep. This called for the labor of
many miners and raised wages for the common people,
and in this way put much money into circulation and
enriched all the people. Cotton mills were built at Pittsburg, Tonganoxie and Lecompton and soon were able
to produce all the cotton goods that the people needed.
Of course, it took much labor to produce the raw cotton
because of the severe climate of the state, but that only
meant more employment and more prosperity. What
the people lacked in cotton goods they made up in employment and prosperity.

The greatest difficulty came after the system of
protection had been in operation in Kansas for some

time, and the people had become prosperous enough to import goods into the state in spite of the tariff. The philosophers of the protectionist school had anticipated this situation, however, for it was the logical result of the policy that they followed. Their solution of the difficulty was to raise the tariff higher; but this was only a makeshift for, of course, the higher they raised the tariff the more prosperous the people became, the more they were able to import, and the higher the tariff had to be raised again. This took so much time that it finally became necessary to create a state tariff commission to attend to the business of raising the tariff. This commission kept statistics of wealth and prosperity and every evening stated how high the tariff would be on the day following. Thus, they avoided the necessity of keeping the legislature in session all of the time.

The beneficial effects of these state customs duties, like the benefits of national protection, proved far greater than anyone had expected. In the first place, these duties provided such abundant revenues that the states were able to provide many agencies for the uplift of the common people such as schools for the development of patriotism, law and order, and the old-fashioned religion and for the building of libraries, museums and monuments. State universities received generous appropriations which enabled them to build better stadia and union buildings in which the students could play and dance and get together; and many universities were enabled to build campaniles with bells and chimes which played *Nearer My God to Thee* on Sunday mornings.

More important even than this, the states were enabled to give higher bounties to industries; and so more industries were built up, more labor was hired, higher wages were paid, more money was put in circulation and kept at home, and the people were blessed and enriched therewith.

The state tariffs, like the national tariffs, had no tendency to reduce interstate trade but, on the contrary, greatly to increase it. As the great Efficiency Engineer Economist had so well demonstrated, trade obstruction has the effect of so increasing the prosperity of the people that they can afford to import even more than before. So the people of each state had far more goods to consume than they had ever had before. They had all the goods they had previously imported—indeed, much more since they were so prosperous—and in addition they had all the goods that were produced by the new industries that the tariff had caused to be established. The people of Kansas, for instance, had all the automobiles they had previously imported from Michigan and all that they now produced in their own factories; they had all the cotton goods they had previously bought from North Carolina and all that they now produced in their factories at Pittsburg, Tonganoxie and Lecompton. This increase in wealth presented a very great moral danger for the people which was happily averted by the teaching of happiness history and by compulsory public training in morals, thrift, patriotism, military marching, citizenship and religion in all the schools and colleges. All of the schools had excellent staffs for teaching such matters.

The very great success which had thus attended the obstruction of interstate trade led to agitation for the creation of additional states by the division of the larger states into two or more states so that more tariffs could be levied and more trade be obstructed. Kansas was divided up into a western and an eastern division, and a high tariff levied on all trade between the two parts which resulted in a great industrial development of the western part of the state. Automobile factories, packing plants, textile mills, shoe factories, etc., etc., were built at Sharon Springs, Syracuse, Goodland and Lenora. On the other hand, this tariff gave a great stimulus to the production of wheat, lean cattle, jack rabbits and broom corn in the eastern part of the state. Tariffs were later imposed at all of the county lines, and this so increased the wealth of Kansas that other states promptly adopted the same policy. The United States was finally divided into three thousand geographical units for the purpose of levying tariffs and enriching the people.

When it was seen how beneficent had been all this trade obstruction, there was much debate as to the fundamental reasons for it; but it was finally agreed by all that the reason was to be found in the great economic principle that had governed the administrations of the Little Pickle President and the Efficiency Engineer Economist—the great principle that the *tariff keeps money at home.* This great principle, like Kepler's Law and the Periodic Law, had been seen vaguely long before; but its full significance was only now apparent.

Throughout these happy, momentous years the commercial chambers were working with the Great Engineer Economist, devising new ways of keeping money at home. They secured laws forbidding all trade with Sears Roebuck and Montgomery Ward; and this stimulated local businesses for a week until Sears Roebuck and Montgomery Ward merged under a new name, "The Farmers' Foundation." Before new laws could be passed on the subject, the Farmers' Foundation had sold its B stock to the farmers of the country; and this prevented further enrichment of the people by this legislation. Similar laws were passed relating to the chain stores, however, and were effective in driving them out of business and bringing back that splendid community builder, the old home grocery store. For a while some people complained that they had to pay higher prices than they had paid when they bought of the chain stores, but it was explained to them that the old-fashioned grocery store did far more to enrich the community than the chain store because it did not take the money out of the community. It was pointed out that when people bought of the chain store the purchaser got the goods but the community lost the money, so there was no real gain from the transaction at all; whereas, when goods were bought from the home groceryman, the purchaser had the goods and the community still had the money. Even if the goods cost more, the community was far better off because it still had the money. The community, so to speak, could eat its cake and have it too.

The commercial chambers not only helped to keep money at home but devoted much energy to bringing industries to the towns and cities so that more money could be kept at home. In Kansas, for instance, the commercial chambers and other boosting orders inaugurated a grand drive to bring industries to the state. A healthy and stimulating competition developed among the various cities seeking such industries. Some offered to buy sites for the new industries; others offered to remit all taxes for a certain number of years; then others offered not only to buy the sites but to put up the buildings; and finally it became the fashion to build the plants, to pay the taxes and to pay part of the salaries of the officials of the companies. Some of the most enterprising of the booster party advocated building homes for the employees of the companies too; but it was impossible to get the people to agree to this.

The result of all this was to raise the population of most of the cities to such figures as to reflect great credit on the agencies which had brought such things to pass. Wichita got a population of more than a million people, Salina half that many, and Dodge City, with the enterprising spirit which characterizes the great untamed West, soon had a million and a half—all boosters—ranking next to Detroit among the great cities of the country. The wealth and prosperity of this great city was founded on the enterprise of her citizens, who offered far more encouragement to industries than any other city of the new West.

This was shown, for instance, in the way that this city secured the glove factory which soon employed 10,000 people. When the officers of the company in New Jersey announced that they wished to expand their business, the delegates of Dodge City promptly informed them that they would guarantee the raw material for the business, would build and provide the machinery for the factory, exempt all its business from taxation for 99 years and give them a cash bonus of 10 per cent of their gross business each year. This was more than Sharon Springs had offered so Dodge City secured the business.

There was much difficulty getting the right kind of

raw material for certain kinds of gloves. The hides of the camels which grew so luxuriantly on the dry plains were too stiff and coarse as were also cow hides; and, of course, kid gloves were impossible since Congress had failed to provide a tariff on goats. But it was presently found that the skins of prairie dogs were admirably suited to use in fine gloves, and a subcommittee of the commercial chamber was appointed to secure the requisite number of these animals. It gave employment to many men and women to chase the prairie dogs over the plains; and, of course, the farther away they had to go to catch the velvet-coated little animals, the more employment it gave and the higher wages were and the more wealth was disseminated among the people of Dodge City.

Good will and trade expansion expeditions were organized by all the commercial chambers, and these brought very great benefit to all. In these expeditions the members of the commercial chambers drove about in their automobiles from town to town saying "Hello" in a friendly way and giving everyone a tin whistle or a lollypop. In Kansas there was much argument about this gift, some asserting that the tin whistle was a better gift and others holding that the lollypop was more appropriate to the occasion and more likely to bring trade to the home town. The debate waxed so spirited that the old party lines between Republicans and Democrats were entirely forgotten, and two new parties emerged—the Tin Whistle Party and the Lollypop Party. This new political alignment brought no bad results since the members of both the Tin Whistle Party and the Lollypop Party were sincerely interested in building up the prosperity of the people.

These commercial chambers also did a great deal to uplift the rural population. They persuaded the farmers to build good roads between the towns; they provided banquets for promising farm boys, sales pavilions where bankrupt farmers could sell their goods and rest rooms for farm women who came to the towns to shop.

The chambers also did much to stimulate the spirit of cheer and happiness. They formed happiness clubs where businessmen got together and discussed the blessings they enjoyed, and these clubs grew so rapidly as to absorb many of the churches. They gave prizes for happiness slogans which were then hung in banners along the streets. The result of this wide dissemination of cheer was such an increase in the health of the people that there was no further need for doctors except the Christian Science doctors who were made special officers of the chambers and of the state.

Thus, by a scientific and thorough-going application of the principles of protection and by keeping money at home, the protectionist party brought great prosperity to the people. It is true that there were a few poor people yet; but they were of the lower classes that were unable or unwilling to exert themselves and rise out of their poverty even with the encouragement that the tariffs offered. Fortunately, the rich and capable classes had gained so much in wealth that they had plenty of money with which to investigate the poor and find out the scientific reasons for their poverty and to give Christmas dinners to those who were found worthy. All this gave much employment to sociologists, gave the poor the bellyache once a year, and gave the rich a comfortable sense of having been generous and charitable without spending enough to corrupt the lower classes or to force any curtailment of their own opportunities for corruption. Thus, the poverty of the poor was a blessing in all respects just as the tariffs were.

So general was the enthusiasm and happiness of the people that when the great Efficiency Engineer Economist's term of office had expired, many of them wanted to make him King or Dictator, like Mussolini; and a great delegation of the United States Commercial Chamber was appointed to call upon him and ask him to take over the government and administer the tariffs. This he was finally persuaded to do on condition that he be allowed to inaugurate a "New Economic Policy" which should represent the final completion and rounding out—the efflorescence, so to speak—of the protectionist program. He explained that while the tariff had been applied logically and consistently to traffic between communities, it had not yet been applied to trade between individuals; and he assured the delegation that by extending the great principle of protection in this way he could further enhance the prosperity and happiness of the people.

In pursuance of this policy, in the first year of his reign as King and Dictator and Regulator and Extender of the Tariffs, the great Efficiency Economist issued an edict taxing all sales, all trade between individuals. He explained to the people that the new order was for the purpose of encouraging industry, providing employment, and increasing wealth, that while it might seem a hardship at first, in the long run, like the tariffs, it would enhance the prosperity of the people so much that they would be able to buy and sell and trade more than ever.

## Excelsior: A Story of Tariff Prosperity

The sales taxes were an unmixed blessing just as the tariffs were. Farmers found that since they paid a tax when they bought shoes they could well afford to make their own shoes. In this way they found employment and kept their money at home. Plumbers found that when they were taxed on the meat they bought they could afford to raise their own chickens and pigs and cows; and this not only meant more employment for plumbers but diversification of industries for the town. Many people found clothing with the tax added too expensive to buy so they made their own clothes. In this way housewives were given employment, the money was kept at home, and all the people blessed and enriched therewith. And, of course, in the long run the farmers bought more shoes, and plumbers bought more meat, and everyone bought more clothing than ever before because everyone was so much more prosperous.

Thus again was encountered the same beneficent circle that was met in the operation of all tariffs. The higher the sales taxes were raised, the more employment people had, the more prosperous they became, the more goods they were able to buy, and the higher the sales taxes had to be raised again. It finally became necessary to create a Government Sales Tax Elevation Commission whose function was to raise the sales taxes each week. Thus, the great Efficiency Engineer Economist had again enriched his people by the application of simple economic principles which had never been understood by the most learned economists; and there was great rejoicing among the people.

But even greater achievements were in store for them for the great Efficiency Engineer Economist, King and Dictator and Regulator and Extender of the Tariffs, issued a second mandate of even more far-reaching importance than the first. Realizing full well that the people might not understand the profound and subtle logic of his scheme, he explained that the sales tax was not fully effective for the reasons above mentioned, that it was essential to all tariff legislation—and, indeed, to all legislation designed to enrich the people—that it must operate to prevent the people from working in the most effective and advantageous way possible, that national tariffs, for instance, were imposed to prevent the world from taking advantage of the economy of international division of labor, that interstate tariffs were useful only as far as they prevented the development of regional or territorial division of labor, and that the sales taxes were enriching the people by reducing occupational division of labor, that once the people had become very prosperous, the sales taxes were no longer fully effective. Therefore, as a supplement to the sales taxes, he was issuing a decree that all specialized occupations should be abolished, that all plumbers should become farmers, that all farmers should sell millinery, that all milliners should teach music and that musicians should run the banks. It was further decreed that every man should change his occupation at least once every month and should trade jobs with his wife at least one day in each week. If he had no wife, he could trade jobs with someone else's wife.

This order aroused much discussion, and there were some who declared that it would ruin the country. But the logic of it gradually permeated the public understanding. The new order provided much more employment since workers could not do as much as formerly and more of them were needed and demanded. This, of course, raised wages and increased the general prosperity. It is true that some of the goods and services offered were not as good as had been available previously; but what the people lacked in goods and services they made up in employment and prosperity—and much more indeed.

But the crowning achievement of the great Efficiency Engineer Economist, King and Dictator and Regulator and Extender of the Tariffs, was still to come; and it followed as a logical climax to the great series of constructive decrees just recorded. In the third year of his reign he issued an order decreeing that all workmen, while engaged in the performance of their duties, should wear hobbles not to exceed one foot in length. As on previous occasions, he explained the philosophy underlying the decree. He pointed out that all of the various laws and decrees imposed during the past years had been designed to prevent the world, the nation and the states from availing themselves of the most economical and effective ways of doing things, that these laws had, in a sense, hobbled and obstructed economic activities to the great benefit and enrichment of the people, and that, obviously, hobbling the people themselves would bring similar benefits.

All this seemed so reasonable that the people cheerfully accepted the new decree and adjusted their hobbles, with hearts grateful for the wise and courageous leadership that God and the Republican Party had given them.

It was soon evident, however, that while the new

decree greatly increased the amount of employment and prosperity, its blessings were unequally distributed, that the hobbles were a far greater benefit to some than to others. They were far more beneficial, for instance, to tall men than to short men, more helpful to farmers and mail carriers who had to walk great distances each day than to professors and chauffeurs who walked very little and therefore received scarcely any benefit at all.

The great Efficiency Engineer Economist finally appointed a commission known as the "Hobbling and Perambulation Interference Investigation Commission" to investigate the injustices in the hobbling regulations and suggest ways of perfecting them. After long deliberation the Hobbling Commission, as it was vulgarly called by the common people, issued an exhaustive scientific report in 25 volumes showing exactly how much benefit each class of people got from various types of perambulatory interference and recommending other ways of interfering with activity. A decree was immediately issued putting these recommendations into effect. In some occupations, workmen were permitted to tie one arm behind them; in others they were required to wear a blinder over one eye; in others they must walk backward; in still others they were required and permitted to stand on their heads. With a beautiful and touching fidelity to the great principle of circulatory obstructionism, brain workers were required to wear their collars at least two sizes too small for them. Thus, each occupation had an appropriate blessing for, like all the decrees of the great Tariff Regulator, this decree was very scientifically drawn.

Thus was the program of protectionism brought to

its logical ultimate perfection. Thus was it brought to flower in new heights of prosperity for God's chosen people. It seemed that there could be no possible further extensions of this great, energizing, wealth-producing principle. But suddenly, without any warning, unforeseen by even the greatest business minds, a cruel depression settled down upon the people. There was much dispute as to how it got into the country. Some said that Bolshevik agents brought it in; others maintained that it came from Europe by way of Honduras in a bunch of bananas. Everyone agreed that it was unfortunate anyhow that the protectionist statesmen had neglected to provide an effective tariff against depressions.

*The characteristic salute of the modern world is a man looking at his wrist watch.*

# NO TIME TO LIVE

*An address delivered at the Unitarian Forum, Kansas City, Missouri, October 7, 1951, and later at various and sundry places.*

Every Thursday I have to write a check for the laundryman. Two or three days later Thursday comes around again, and I have to write another check, and I am always puzzled as to what has happened to the other days that are supposed to be in the weekly calendar. I seem to have slept over most of them, for in Kansas I could not, of course, have been enjoying a bender. These weeks are my life, for life is made up of weeks, and I seem to find little in them—except my classes which are a great joy—that I can remember as worthwhile or significant. This adds up to the conclusion that, aside from my classes, my life is pretty dull, meaningless, for the most part, and that some day I will find that I have used up my allotment of time and won't be able to figure out what I have got out of it—my life, the only one I am quite sure of.

The years slip by in the same way. A year looks like a lot of days, a stretch of time long enough to get some real kick out of life and, perhaps, to do something worthwhile. Yet I find that I just about finish dismantling the Christmas tree when I have to go poking around in the closets to find the decorations again. How many years can pass in a little while, pass almost unnoticed and unsung!

A few years ago I had two little boys, dear little boys. (The neighbors called them ornery brats, but they didn't understand them.) I enjoyed my little boys more than most men do, I believe, because I had a presentiment that they would grow up and be gone some day—some day far in the future. Twenty years ought to be a long time, a time full of good fun with the boys. But I awoke a year or so later to find the boys grown up, graduated, gone out into the big world to repeat the mistakes I had made.

Twenty years! What had I done with them? What did I get out of them? They went by so fast that I had only time to blink at each one, no time to sample the golden hours as they passed. No time for anything but work and trivialities, that seems to be my trouble; and it is a common complaint of busy men, those who can sit still long enough to think enough to complain.

Why have we so little time? Where does it go? Or, rather, why isn't 24 hours enough? I never had more than that, but I can remember when I had *time* —long Sunday afternoons when I could read books undisturbed and with no feeling that there were a dozen other things I should be doing; evenings that seemed like whole evenings to play the piano or sing or read or in winter to study my lessons. It was an unhurried life we led, more than a generation ago. We had only a few good friends, and when we visited them we stayed much of the day—a leisurely day that did not fly past like a tumbleweed in an April wind.

When we went to Lawrence to college we did not expect to make the trip in four hours but rode the unhurried Central Branch, changed trains a time or two, making connections if we were lucky, if not, lounging around the depot for some hours or perhaps all night. I remember well the evening my sister and I missed connections at Beloit and sat out behind the depot most of the night, reciting poetry and talking of our plans and ambitions and theories of the good life. It was full moon, and there was a mist on the field of ripening wheat across the fence, and the frogs were croaking from the creek nearby. Sister has been gone these many years, but I can close my eyes and see that lovely, peaceful scene as if I had been there only yesterday. An interruption of our journey which I, no doubt, cursed with vigor had enriched my life with an unforgettable experience. It was enforced leisure but how rich and enduring.

Some classes of people probably have more leisure than they used to have. The vast productivity of modern industry has made it possible to reduce the work day of laborers, and they doubtless have more leisure. In the home, the washing and ironing machines, dishwashers, disposalls, electric toasters, mixers, percolators, sweepers, waxers—a score of machines of various kinds—have provided leisure for the housewife, no doubt; and if we could just invent a machine for raising the children, she would have more freedom than the Constitution guarantees. But even the housewife may and sometimes does take up bridge or culture and uplift clubs until she too has no time. Most of the housewives I see complain that they have only one pair of hands and so can't get their necessary work done.

It is the middle and upper classes, the business and professional men, who find the stress of life growing. Businessmen must be better, more efficient than they were a generation ago, must work harder; doctors and lawyers and teachers must be and are better trained, which means long years of exacting training and hard work throughout life. For these classes the machines have brought no free time, no leisure. The automobile could be used to cut down the time needed to go places and so provide more leisure time, but it seems merely to make us think of more places to go. Measured in miles or in the speed with which we cover them, ours is a rich life; measured in significant things done, it verges on pauperism. On fine spring or fall days, for instance, we start out on a round of calling with a bag of calling cards; and two hours later return home to find an equal number of cards piled up around the front door. A philosopher friend of mine says that his hardest problem is to avoid most of the social contacts that modern transportation makes possible.

So the machines haven't provided leisure. On the contrary, they produce so much of so many things that we feel impelled to hurry to get the money to buy and the time to enjoy as much as possible. There are too many things that we can do, too many things to want, too many kinds of entertainment, too many ways of spending time; but why should this not be the happiest situation imaginable? Too many things, too many ways of enjoying ourselves, that's an odd complaint to make. One trouble is that so many of the goods are shoddy, so much of the entertainment we should be ashamed of.

Another difficulty is that this avalanche of goods has
to be sold; and so Americans have become a nation of
salesmen and advertisers, beating the drums, banging
the cymbals, blowing the trumpets, hammering the bells,
shouting the refrain: buy Camel cigarettes, buy the
bright beer, buy Calvert whisky and become a distinguished man, buy a Longines watch, buy a Crosley refrigerator, buy a Parker pen, buy Cape Cod crystal, buy
a Zenith radio, buy Oxydol, Dreft, Drene, Lux, Windex,
Hex, Coca Cola, buy Camay soap or Palmolive and take
a bath, or buy Mum or Arrid and you won't have to. Buy
a Ford car, Firestone tires, Skelly gasoline, Autolite
spark plugs, and drive to the Regal Inn, order a dinner
of Swift's Premium ham, Del Monte peas, Wonder
bread, Velvet ice cream; then drive home, take a Bayer's
aspirin and Alka Seltzer and go to sleep on your Sealy
mattress at the end of a perfect day. Buy, buy, buy Lawrence, buy Wichita, buy Republican, buy patriotism,
loyalty, success, friends, poise, polish—anything and everything but peace and quiet and inner contentment. I
wonder how long it will be before we will buy Salvation
as sponsored by Super Duper Suds. I believe that Americans have no idea how they have been debauched by
this incessant clatter, how they have lost sight of intellectual and spiritual values, how they have become
about the world's most shallow and superficial mate-
rialists, working themselves into diabetes and hardened
arteries and high blood pressure to pile up mountains of
largely meaningless odds and ends of tinseled trash, like
so many pack rats or jackdaws, giving not a moment's
thought to the problem of choosing what they themselves would like to get out of life, buying what everyone
else is buying, running with the thoughtless pack, and

never stopping long enough to wonder what the crazy marathon is all about.

So great is the pressure to take in as many sorts of entertainment as possible that we often try to enjoy several at the same time. So, at breakfast, I turn on the radio to get the news, read the newspaper, eat what I assume is my breakfast, and rub the dog with my foot under the table on the theory that the dog must be entertained too, perhaps also carrying on a desultory conversation with my wife who is reading the *Ladies Home Journal* and pedaling the other side of the dog. So we have to listen to the car radio while driving, talk or read or do both while listening to the radio concert and, on the side, perhaps try to figure out whether we can afford a new rug. It is impossible for Americans to sit and listen to a mere radio or record concert. They must talk; indeed, the beginning of the concert is the signal for the babbling to begin. Have you ever tried to turn the radio louder on such an occasion? Well, this forces the conversation to a higher pitch which calls for more volume on the radio until one gets a fair reproduction of the Haymarket riot.

We must save time even though the more we save the less we seem to have. Railway trains go some 50 per cent faster than they did 30 years ago; airplanes set new records every few months as if this were a great civilizing achievement; every year the highway departments straighten and shorten the roads here and there, perhaps saving as much as five minutes of our precious time. Recently in one of New York's passenger stations, a conveyor belt was installed which will save commuters an average of 20 seconds every time they leave the station. Surely ours is a century of wonders!

Americans have developed such speed and zest in their work that they are generally incapable of enjoying leisure. They must make work of it. So the tired businessman of my town, facing a 2-weeks vacation, jumps into his car after supper, drives 650 miles to Denver overnight, and on up to Cheyenne where there is a rodeo, then up into the mountains where he whips the mountain streams for a week or two as if his life depended on the number of fish he could catch, then drives home at 70 miles an hour, arriving in such condition that it takes a week of work to restore his vitality. So, as Bernard DeVoto once said: "The United States contains millions of people who will drive from Hartford to Seattle and back by way of Los Angeles in three weeks, with a 9-year-old and a 6-year-old in the rear seat, and at the end will be in practically as good condition as their car . . . . Three weeks at a popular summer resort are hardly more destructive to their health and morale than divorce, bankruptcy, or a nervous breakdown; they take the experience in their stride, shrug it off, and in a few months are completely restored." In my own family, last Christmas my two sons, reared, if you please, in a philosophical atmosphere, employed their 2-weeks vacation in driving home from San Francisco to Lawrence, Kansas, in two days, sleeping and visiting a few days, then driving back to San Francisco by way of Mexico City. Wonderful vacation! I confess that I'm guilty of such things myself. On Saturdays I sometimes go out to work in my yard just for leisurely exercise and enjoyment, but I often find myself presently hurrying as if the sheriff were after me. Work in the American tradition, not leisure!

But we *must* work hard at our leisure in order to

consume the vast flood of gilded and tinseled goods that pour from the assembly lines, or they will pile up on us and bring depression—as President Eisenhower has perhaps noticed. We can't relax for a moment or the economy becomes clogged with "surplus goods"—the economists call them "inventories." In spite of our pertinacious pumping of the accelerator, cars, new and second-hand, have been piling up in the yards and show rooms until they look to the dealers like an invasion of locusts. On my way west last summer I think I saw 500 square miles of second-hand cars rusting in the June sunshine and more new cars than a sensible people would buy or would have time to drive. Of course, war, the great destroyer, is a help here; but unfortunately it destroys men as well as goods so we hope we won't have war.

According to capitalist standards of morality, leisure is a sin anyhow. We must *succeed*, and we don't succeed by enjoying leisure. I can imagine a typical ambitious father saying good-bye to his son who, after graduation, is going out to seek his fortune. "My dear son, you are on your own now, but I hope you will hold fast to the traditions of your father. Remember that life is real, life is earnest, and success is its goal. Don't ever do anything merely because you want to for that won't lead you anywhere. It is true that you might enjoy it, but forget about that.

"If you are to succeed you must do mostly hard work, the things that you don't want to do; and if you do such things for 50 years, you may be a very famous man, perhaps a millionaire or a congressman or a diplomat or a writer of books; or at any rate you may pile up enough of a fortune to endow your widow for her second husband after heart disease has taken you off and you

have become the richest man in the cemetery. Life is
for work, and not vice versa. Early to bed and early
to rise, as Benjamin Franklin said; and they're good for
you, my son, because you don't like either one. At any
rate I hope, my dear boy, that you'll be a success whether you enjoy your life or not."

Years ago my first boy started to school; and as I
saw him trudging away down the street, turning to wave
at us, I thought sadly: "He's stepping into the treadmill,
poor boy, and he'll never get out of it until the glass wag-
on carries him off."

The emulative spirit is, of course, a ruthless destroyer of leisure. We must keep up with the Joneses;
and here they are flaunting their new cars and fur coats
and nylons before us, cheapening everything we have,
sowing in our hearts the seeds of envy and malice where
Christian brotherhood ought to reign. Modern cars, radios, television, movies and advertising make us more
conscious of what they have. Leslie James says that
the Joneses is American slang for the Trinity; but I wish
that outfit would move to New Caledonia or Borneo for
they are a worse nuisance than the Jukes or the Kallikaks, or perhaps even than the communists. The Joneses
have destroyed more wealth than all the tornadoes, cyclones, floods, Japanese beetles and grasshoppers in
America, have caused more unhappiness than love, divorce, influenza and obesity. We see this numerous,
ubiquitous outfit wherever we go, and they always make
us unhappy and compel us to work when we would
rather enjoy our leisure. The FBI should rid us of this il-
lustrious but pestiferous family.

We are all in this conspiracy to stir up the emulative
spirit. We spend much of our time picking out and el-

evating to supreme honor and dignity certain individuals for the less fortunate to envy and emulate. So we choose every year the "Mother of the Year," the supercolossal, supermaternal, superangelic m o t h e r, the one out of some 30,000,000 who towers over all others like the Statue of Liberty over the hurrying crowds of New York, like Saint Cabrini over the sinful unanointed. Can we not hear each of the other 29,999,999 mothers crying: "What have I done? What have I failed to do? Wherein have I failed to measure up?" And then: "Well, next year I will plan and work and pray and fast and try to do better. I wonder what my rank was this year." I cannot help wondering how the committee could have known 30,000,000 mothers well enough to make a wise choice.

So, about every year we choose Miss America, the very most beautiful, charming, entrancing, alluring and revealing young lady in the land. So, in the University we used to ferret out the "Honor Man of the Year"—the one honorable man in four or five thousand. One year we would pick out a football hero, the next a violinist, the next year the most eminent or notorious student politician. So too we have queens for all the festivals of importance. So do some cities select the "Man of the Year," or the "Most Useful Citizen," or some such celebrity; the Rotary Club and every club single out a most eminent or useful or distinguished member; some group of experts names the "Master Farmers" or "Star Farmers of America"; the Boys Club of America chooses the "Boy of the Year"; the United States Chamber of Commerce democratically designates the "Ten Outstanding Young Men of the Year." Not long ago the Women's National Aeronautics Association found and proclaimed the "Woman of the Year"; the American Association of University Women names the "Outstanding Senior Woman in the University." Recently, I noticed that Ottawa University had discovered and named the two "Most Representative Students" of the University—surely a very great honor.

Competition is indeed the life of trade, the beneficent regulator of price, quality and service in business. It is competition that brings us groceries of high quality at moderate prices, although it also brings some grocerymen to an untimely end with heart disease and hardened arteries; but why should the competitive spirit be so pertinaciously projected into our social life, to make that as hurried and as strenuous and competitive as business? Why can't we be allowed to live quietly and unostentaciously away from our business? Is it impossible that we should do our fair share of good deeds without the hope of being chosen the most useful or most honorable or most distinguished man or woman of the town, the Chamber of Commerce or the Rotary Club? Perhaps a nation without orders of nobility craves that sort of thing, but it takes time and energy, and I think it's silly.

To further sop up our spare time we have parades and festivals and dedications. At the University we have several annual parades in addition to the shirt-tail football parade and the commencement parades. We must dedicate each new building, I don't quite understand why, and every new chancellor has also to be dedicated by half a dozen organizations downtown. And when chancellors and deans and even sometimes professors reach the age when they must totter off into retirement and obscurity, we often dedicate them in reverse, make speeches about their "years of service"—which unkind critics sometimes refer to as "years at the public trough." Some time each year we have Engineers Day and Business Day with festivities and perhaps parades and queens—something to keep the students' minds off their lessons. Downtown every spring and fall, we have an "opening" of the stores, apparently to show the people where the stores are and how they can be opened.

The American habit of joining organizations must bear a major share of the responsibility for our busyness, our lack of leisure. We are great "joiners." Now, organization often seems to be necessary to accomplish certain noble ends. We seem to have to have a separate organization for the protection of every negro who is being railroaded to the electric chair, for the protection of share croppers, racial minorities, children, wild life, redwood trees—about everything. In some organizations there may be a modest amount of enlightening and cultural discussion, but many organizations have little purpose but to get together and waste time—to enable people who have no ideas and no desire for ideas and nothing worth while to say to get together with other people who have no ideas and no desire for ideas and nothing to say and to pass the evening without being reminded that nothing significant is said. They do take a lot of time.

There are many human microbes in this world who find their chief joy in forming new organizations to take other people's time, and we must resist their wiles for they hit us from two directions. They force us to earn the money for dues, and then they want us to come to their meetings. If we would have time, we must use DDT on these fellows. Of course, they call it "fellowship," but fellowship can be spread too thin; and organized activity violates what is to me a sacred right —the right to do what I want to do when I want to do it. These meetings begin at a certain time, and everything occurs on a specified time. (The characteristic salute of the modern world is a man looking at his wrist watch.) After meeting my classes on time, I like to do some other things when I please. That makes me feel like an individual and not a member of a society of termites.

There are so many student organizations at most universities that many students have little time for study or for the sleep that knits up the raveled sleeve of care; they are so busy with all the scatter-brained activities that do murder sleep. It is fortunate that we have classes, for our classes provide ideal conditions for sleep —hard mental work and the somnolent hum of the professor's voice.

I believe it isn't mainly the lessons that keep our students so busy and so tired. If it were, they would be most exhausted on Friday; but they are always most fatigued and exhausted on Monday morning after a 2-day holiday, or even worse, on the first day after a 2-weeks vacation. They are so very busy; and I wonder if many of them aren't gladly throwing away their lives, week by week, and getting little solid satisfaction from them. Consider the student calendar. Monday, "Well, I have a tough week ahead. Hope I can make it." Friday, "Oh, I made it. Thank God this week's over." So, do they not "Thank God this week's over" every week of the term; and then "Thank God, that term's over"; and at the end of the year, "Thank God that year's over. It was surely a tough year." They seem to be thankful that their lives are slipping rapidly past—which seems to suggest suicide as the logical course for them.

We professors also have too many organizations. I once counted 77 regular committees of the University and about an equal number of special committees. Some professors serve on as many as eight or ten committees and yet try to do some teaching on the side. Most committee meetings are very dull for there is usually nothing worth while to do; and in my own University, some professors bring their knitting to the sessions since they are not permitted to read. If they should happen to have a little time left over from academic duties, they are likely to feel obliged to spend it at the University Club or at meetings of the Rotary Club, the City Council, the Flower Club, the Association for the Advancement of Eurasian Culture, or the Committee for the Industrial Development of the Sand Hills of Sukanatchee County.

It is sometimes argued that many of the people who buy the cheap, standardized goods, listen to the cheap, standardized radio and television dramas, drive their shiny standardized cars past our billboards from one organization to another do not care for anything better, would not be happy with anything better, that if they had to buy fewer goods and finer or were obliged to stop moving for an hour, they would be bored to tears. Conceded, for the present, but the flood of goods that have to be bought and the perpetual motion of our whirling dervishes are, to some extent, the cause of our cultural aridity. We might have to slow down a little or perhaps even sit quiet occasionally to develop better taste. One can't think very deeply at 70 miles an hour. If we could slow down a little and read something worth while, we might even learn enough about economics and politics and international affairs to save American democratic civilization. Up to now we can't say that we are doing that.

"Go to the ant, thou sluggard." Yes, if you want a perfect replica of American economic society, go to the ant. All the ants I ever saw were just running around in a feverish hurry, rushing hither and yon, perhaps with worthless pebbles in their jaws which they dropped where they would do the least good, then starting off in another direction for other baubles, or perhaps with no apparent purpose at all but to keep in training. They do, of course, manage to dig a hole in the ground (Americans build skyscrapers instead); and they seem to rear their young; but their progeny grow up to be just as crazy as the parents. I never saw an ant sit down and think; he just runs round like a lunatic—or an American. The American patriotic emblem should be the ant rather than the eagle.

Well, what can we do about it? Is there any way of simplifying life to a point where we can have a little *time*? In a profit-motivated society, we can hardly expect a shift from quantity to quality in the flood of goods, newspapers, magazines, music, drama and books. Profit must be served, and there is usually profit in the shoddy stuff. The best we can do is to pick and choose, on the theory that it takes less time to choose the little really good than try to digest the entire output.

This is about my own greatest problem, but I am making a little progress. Of goods I usually buy little— of the best that I can afford. In the newspapers I have narrowed my interests down to the significant national and international news, to such great outstanding figures as Cohn and McCarthy. I have long saved some precious time by ignoring the sports page. I would rather play myself than read about someone else playing. I don't spend much time reading about the poor little boy who fell in the well and got wet and would have drowned if the water had been deeper or about the ambitious young man who started out on a shoestring and wound up with a million shoestrings and coronary thrombosis. I know those stories by heart.

Perhaps a social policy of income equalization would help us a little. A steeply graduated income tax, if efficiently collected, would reduce the incentive for work among the classes that tend most to overwork. It would tend to distribute more widely the opportunities for distinctive work. A steeply progressive tax on the high incomes might well reduce the incentive for excessively hard work, distribute the important work among a larger number of men, perhaps without lowering the quality of services appreciably. It is rather too advantageous to be a big shot in our present economy, and too few have the opportunity to be big shots. If less of the money, power and glory of modern life were accorded to the few at the top, there would be less of a scramble to get to the top; and more people might have a little time.

I have always found new books one of my hardest problems; have been buying the books that I *ought* to read, then putting them up on the shelves to be read in a future of abundant leisure that never comes. There on the shelves they stand glaring at me reproachfully, reminding me that I shall have no free time until they are read. This year, however, I am in sight of a solution— giving a thousand books to the University, which may be able to find some readers. As to new books, I find that I can save time by going through the book cata-

logues, marking the books that I want, and throwing the
catalogues into the waste basket. There are a few
people, not many, who read too many books.

There are a few other ways of saving precious time.
A really good book read aloud and discussed with the
family at the dinner table raises the tone of the dinner,
although it is difficult to manage with a full mouth. I
have read some of Shakespeare and a lot of Mark Twain
in this way. A book would not need to be very good to
run somewhat above the ordinary dinner table conversation.

And I am no longer a joiner. I think we must be individualists, stubborn individualists if we are to have
any time. We must learn to enjoy being thought a bit
crazy, perhaps even somewhat impolite.

For instance, it is a fashion to send out Christmas
cards to all our relatives, friends, acquaintances and
some strangers in various parts of the world from Siberia
to Guadalcanal. In my timid youth I fell in with the
fashion until I had to fix up a card index to keep track
of my friends and was on the point of engaging a secretary to manage the business. Then a great light fell upon
me, and I sent a notice to several hundred thousand
people that I was their very dear friend, loved them and
would treasure their love and friendship until further notice, that in the meantime would they please put my
name down as a friend and think of me at Christmas
time or as soon thereafter as convenient and practicable,
as I would also vice versa and reciprocally, but that I
would not spend two weeks before the birthday of the
Prince of Peace getting out enough Woolworth cards to
give the mailman arthritis for *His* Christmas. Oh, I do
care for my friends, and I reply to all such cards if I can,

but not in Christmas vacation. And I don't just send the printed lines about the joys of the non-existent peace but tell them how I am and my wife and the boys and the dog—something intimate and confidential. Similarly, I long ago dropped the custom of giving anyone but the children Christmas presents. If it's the *custom,* I'm against it, particularly since by being so I can save money and time.

Like most men, I find that as I grow older I take on some new functions and new responsibilities; but I am learning to choose. I'm learning that most of what I do is of little importance. I'm making progress, and perhaps I may solve my problem. If I can't do it in some way, I suspect that heart disease and hardened arteries and high blood pressure will do it for me.

# TOO MUCH AND TOO POOR

*Written merely for relaxation but presented in modified form before the Institute of Consumers' Union of the United States, Kansas State College, July 8, 1952.*

Many, many years ago when I was about five years young, I and my sister, two years younger, were one day sizing up the dumplings in our soup, each claiming to have the largest one. It seemed to us a very important matter; but as we were digging the dumplings out of the soup and comparing them as to size and splendor, each arguing for his or her own specimen, my mother noticed us and laughed disparagingly at our rivalry, much to our embarrassment.

Here were two children already touched with the American spirit and ideals, both anxious to have the biggest of something even if only a dumpling, ridiculed by a parent who, although imbued with the American spirit and ideals of thrift, self-reliance, free enterprise, and rugged individualism, could not see that her little children were looking upward and forward, groping haltingly for the ideals that were destined to make America great and fine and strong.

But 60 years later, I believe I can discern wisdom in my mother's risibility and can do a little smiling on my own at the American stress on size or numbers and the indifference to quality. In fact, I wonder if it is not one of our worst American vices.

We seem always concerned about size or numbers.

"How is your town progressing?"

"Wonderful! Couldn't be better! Population doubled in the last ten years. Wonderful progress! It's lots bigger!"

"Is there any advantage in that?"

A blank stare of incomprehension.

"Hell, man! Do you come from Russia?"

"No, I come from Tonganoxie. But is your town beautiful, has it eliminated slums or retarded areas or cleaned out any of the mountains of junk and rubbish, the broken-down jalopies and streetcars and rusty boilers and tin cans that mark your progress toward metropolitan size and dignity?"

"Oh, yes. I guess the women have been sweating about some of those things. Women have to be busy with something."

"What about education here—"

"Oh, a lot of it—enrollment up 20 per cent last year —had to build two new schools, fine schools!"

"Do you permit educational work in your schools, or are they just for show?"

"Wait a minute there! We pay high salaries and get the best teachers money will buy. Of course, we don't allow any communistic or socialistic teaching or any New Deal stuff. Won first place in football last year."

"You have a college here, I see."

"Yeah, a good one too—bigger than Punkville this year and beat 'em in football. Got a new president last year and he's a live wire, a dynamo—raised the enrollment 12 per cent in one year and brought the football team up from practically nothing to one of the best in the state. Scored 212 points this year."

"I see some nice churches, too."

"Yes sirree! And some preachers who are real boosters. We put on a membership drive this spring and raked in 400 new members and built two new churches and a vestibule, and a gymnasium in one of them so the boys can practice in good moral surroundings and get in shape for the team. Can't start 'em too early, you know. Churches in this town are up and steppin', my friend. Shows what can be done if everybody gets behind and boosts."

Here we see the American obsession with size and numbers. It applies to about everything. In the first place, every state and every city, town and hamlet big enough to boast a post office, a service station and a Rotary Club has a Chamber of Commerce whose main function is to boost the population by enticing the people of other cities and towns to come and abide there. They also seek conventions on the theory that some of the conventioners, seeing what a prosperous and beautiful town they have, may come and buy homes and raise real-estate values.

In a noble effort to raise its population, every state tries to entice the citizens of other states to come within its borders and sometimes waylays and imprisons them to keep them there, somewhat as the Indians once made war on neighboring tribes to capture their women, and as on the early ranges cattle rustlers pounced upon unwary cattle that roamed too far from home. Occasionally, this interstate rivalry brings unfortunate consequences. Along the Texas-Oklahoma border, men and women and children are sometimes torn limb from limb by contending boosters, the legs perhaps going to one state and the arms to the other. Such dismembered persons, somewhat strangely, are included in the statistics of population which accounts for the fact that population figures appear in fractions—legs and torso, arms and head, each counting as one-half person.

Usually the struggle for more population is not carried on with such determination and ferocity but more humanely by state "booster brigades," which use mere psychological appeals, advertising and meretricious chicanery. These "booster brigades" spend large sums of money advertising the virtues of the home state, the magnificent scenery, the deep, rich soil, the limitless natural resources—such as hardpan, useful in making pottery, and rocks valuable as building materials—the energizing and invigorating climate, the vast schools of fish in the streams and lakes, the savage and succulent game awaiting the huntsman, the noble and prosperous cities, the friendly men and virtuous and therefore somewhat less friendly women, the churches and schools and athletic teams and other cultural agencies. Mainly the "booster brigades" point out the vast opportunities for achieving material wealth.

Why should the people want their states and cities and towns to grow? Why do they want to have more people about them when they commonly don't like most of those already there? More and more of those who can afford such luxury seek homes in the suburbs where there are not many people near; yet they appear to want many people to live in other parts of the town as far away as possible. Most of the people of the better classes do not like laborers. They regard them as loafers, malingerers, mostly communists and generally undesirable; yet they strive unceasingly to get new industries to come so they can have laborers around, not too near, to quarrel with. Or, perhaps the laborers do afford utility by providing the better classes with a lower class to feel superior to, thus giving superiority its appropriate setting.

Perhaps the great zeal for attracting neighbors is in part a survival of pioneer days when the settlers were lonely and even welcomed peddlers and preachers to break the monotony of life. They still do love crowds at times—at Fourth of July celebrations, parades and football games, for instance; yet on the other hand, they appear to want to be apart and exclusive most of the time. Apparently they have not worked out any consistent philosophy on this question.

No doubt another reason for the American booster spirit is that Americans are intellectual adolescents, and adolescents quite naturally want to grow. Children grow, *must* grow to achieve adult size, and so they naturally *want* to grow. Indeed, they measure their progress in terms of physical growth, just as Americans in their cities and states do; but when they reach maturity they should turn to other ideals.

Perhaps the main reason for state and city boosterism, however, is that an increasing population tends to raise real-estate values. As a result of their historical conditioning, Americans are land value animals. For 300 years they have been moving westward seeking titles to land that they hoped would rise in value; for

300 years they have been following the lure of the unearned increment, the beacon light of "something for nothing," boosting, bragging, puffing, whoopin' 'er up for the home town and the home state, hoping to sell real estate at an advance. Here we can see the reason for the characteristic American mendacity in such matters. In some matters we are an honest people, but in boosting the home town or state we throw truth and honesty to the winds, and lie, blatantly, shamelessly, without a blush. Boosting shades naturally into lying for it is not only permissible but most honorable to lie about the home town or the home state.

With our great technological efficiency, we produce too much of a great many things. Of food we produce so much that the government agencies are constantly struggling to keep the output down, largely without success, so that the government must buy the surplus and destroy it or give it away. Even so, many of us consume too much, as a result of which obesity has outstripped tuberculosis as our number one health hazard. Two minutes in the mouth, two hours in the stomach, and 20 years under the belt is the story of too many dinners. For the millions of us who are fighting obesity, our plenty of good food offers little satisfaction. We are somewhat in the position of Tantalus, who was condemned to stand hungry and thirsty in water up to his chin, under a tree laden with fruit. Knowing that the refrigerator is crammed with food and that I can afford all I want, I sit down without joy to my 1,100 daily calories in foods most of which I don't like. A Hindu coolie, who never had more than 1,100 calories and therefore likes whatever he can get, sits down to the same amount of food with thankful heart and enjoys it. Just where is the advantage of having abundance of food if you dare not eat it?

Of clothes we have plenty, perhaps fortunately of generally poor materials since style changes make us throw much of our clothing away before it has seen much service, unless we have the moral stamina to ignore the style arbiters. I have some 40 or 50 ties of various designs, enough to last me until I reach the age of about 110. But now the designers have decreed new styles of ties, and I suppose I should throw my old ties away. I shall not do this. I shall wear those ties as long as I live, and one of them to my funeral. I'll have the world know that I set the styles; and if the rest of the yokels don't follow my styles, that is their misfortune.

Of houses we have had too few in most towns, but I can see a surplus emerging over the next hill. In recent years a style of houses has swept the country, making older houses, however beautiful and comfortable, as out-of-date as the moon-decorated cottages of yesterday's back yards. We will not be really contented until every family has a ranch-style house with three or four tiled bathrooms, radio, television and charcoal grills in every room, with walls of every color of the rainbow or of glass, and older houses abandoned. But these styles will not last long; and these houses will, in turn, have to be abandoned. Changing styles seem destined to bring us too many houses although we must concede that our houses are not as big as they used to be when wealthy men could show their solvency only by building big homes.

Our great industrial plants vomit vast quantities of standardized, chrome-plated, tinsel-wrapped goods onto the market—so much that from time to time they must close or slow down or instigate a strike unless they can find relief in war or until consumers catch up with the flood. As Leslie James has said: "When Americans fall behind in their consuming, and surpluses do begin to accumulate, they must drop everything and build skyscrapers. These are the only buildings in which surpluses can be stored without taking up all the room there is in America."[1] It is true that some consumers of the lower classes who want and need some of these things, do not have them—electric refrigerators and decent houses, for instance—and would buy if they had the money; but, of course, it is dangerous to give the lower classes much money.

There are many things—gadgets, gimcracks, gewgaws, inane superfluities that make no difference one way or the other. Of such things there is always too much and too poor: face creams and soaps and face builders and restorers and hair glorifiers and lipsticks —why do women think bloody lips are beautiful?—and shampoos and hair tonics and vibrators and cigar lighters and cocktail sets and hassocks and sandwich toasters —oh, a thousand electric gimcracks—and sport shirts and laxatives and tonics and sedatives and cokes and cold cures. What mountains, what avalanches of largely worthless stuff! But many of our citizens think this shows how fine our civilization is.

In almost everything there are quite too many types and styles. We used to have a choice among a score or so of styles of watches. Today there are hundreds of styles. We used to be thankful if we could afford a white bath tub, for all bath tubs were white;

_____
[1] Leslie James, *Americans in Glasshouses*, p. 42.

now we can choose a variety of colors and styles. A wholesale automobile agent tells me that he has to invest about a million dollars to have at hand all the various parts of all the makes and issues of cars. An optometrist estimates that there are perhaps 2,500 different styles, sizes and colors of spectacle frames. One of his customers bought 12 different styles and colors, one to match each of her dresses! For her kitchen, the housewife can now choose among several colors for her refrigerator, stove, sink, and storage cabinets and combine them in any way that suits her fancy. Such variety scarcely seems essential to a good life, and it certainly adds to the cost of living.

Many common American products are probably as good as those produced anywhere; but in the field of recreation and cultural activities our oversupply of cheap goods and services is conspicuously in evidence and most destructive. There are really too many automobiles, and they are used too much. Automobiles can be useful machines, properly used, but driven at 70 miles an hour on many errands of the most infinitesimal consequence, perhaps for no purpose but to give a nitwit a sense of doing something, they are a hazard and nuisance to those who have something worth while to do. So our holiday traffic looks like an emergency hurry-up funeral procession and always does indeed provide the material for a few hundred funerals the next day. Our national parks are cluttered up with thousands of dolts who go not to see nature's masterpieces but merely to drive somewhere and, once there, crowd the speed limit to get past the scenery as fast as possible. Like the woman I overheard at the rim of the Grand Canyon: "A hell of a ditch! Let's go and get something to eat." When we go down town to shop or to the theater, we are lucky to find parking space closer than our homes. Too many cars! Too much driving. We are a machine-using, machine-worshipping people. We simply wallow in machinery; but the machines have not added greatly to the richness of life; and they have brought us no leisure, no free time.

Movies present even a worse situation—vastly too many and too poor—so many that only a strong man could stand the strain of viewing them all; and only a very stupid man would want to. I do not go to many movies; but once a certain famous movie was being shown in Lawrence, second showing; and my wife and I argued and cudgeled our brains trying to decide whether we had seen it or not. We never did decide. If we had seen it, it must have made a very strong impression. Try to remember the titles and plots of a score of movies, and you will realize what a shallow dent they make on your mind. Too many movies even if they were good, and there's no way of making so many movies good.

I commonly hear, "No, I don't care about seeing that. I'm pretty sure I saw it once." "Pretty sure I saw it once!" When *Macbeth* comes to the city, do we say, "Oh no, I saw that once"? Yet I think we would if Shakespeare had promoted a drama corporation and had turned out 2,000 plays in 20 years. When I hear Brahms' *First Symphony*, I really do not turn the radio off, saying, "I've heard that before," because Brahms wrote only four symphonies, all supremely good, and not a thousand, all supremely bad. "Too much and too poor" describes too much of our cultural and recreational provender, but the stuff takes our precious time.

Indulging in it, the people remind me of cattle eating straw in a hard winter, working full time but losing weight steadily.

Perhaps there are not too many radios for they afford a few useful services. They have done much to give vitality to American political life; and they broadcast news, objective enough if it relates to unimportant questions, much of it badly slanted where it covers important political questions. In general, the radio programs are too many and many of them unbelievably poor. Soap operas, humor so sad that clackers are hired to laugh at it, drama dripping in blood and gore, advertising the FBI, advertising George Washington, patriotism, Americanism and reaction, liver conditioners, breath sweeteners, stomach alkalizers, skin clarifiers, nose and throat pacifiers, mild cigarettes and viciously potent gasoline, perfumes that shade from seduction to assault and battery: these constitute the daily drone of the American radio—intellectual provender for morons. Think of the gain if we could have half as many programs twice as good, or one-fourth as many programs four times as good! Television seems destined to add little cheer to the picture, for most of the programs are perhaps on a lower plane than radio programs and the advertising almost nauseating. Surely such programs must make people mentally lazy if they do nothing worse. Perhaps our scientists may some day be discussing the question: "Why are most Americans idiots?"

Too many clubs and lodges, too, some of them devoted to noble purposes; but there are too many of them. Overproduction, overproliferation a p p l i e s to churches too; and they are mostly poor, in treasury and in the quality of their entertainment. Even in small towns there must be at least a half dozen churches pointing the way to Heaven by a half dozen routes which, on examination, prove to be much the same. The few members must skimp to pay the expenses; the ministers live a life of financial harassment on hod-carriers' wages, exhorting congregations as small as the sermons are generally poor, if better than can rightly be expected; the volunteer choirs sing of the Heavenly choirs of which their performances are only faintly suggestive; the churches are cold in winter, generally uncomfortable and uninspiring and the dinners poor. Here we have competition gone wild.

It may seem fanciful to mention books and magazines among the recreational and cultural resources of America, for Americans, after they leave school, do not read anything worth while. Indeed very few of them, perhaps 5 per cent, *can* read anything good. We do publish vast numbers of books, some 12,000 every year; and the United States leads the world in number of libraries, with 6,100 public libraries and 98,000 school libraries; but most Americans read only a few of the worst of the books. Too many and too poor describes our book provender. So many are there that the reader often gives up the task of choosing what to read and joins a book club or reads the condensations of the *Reader's Digest.*

In magazines, our situation is worse. Some 1,231 different magazines are published of which about 1,100 are pictorial or salacious and pornographic. Too many and too poor! What a boon it would be if all writers of books and magazine articles could take time enough, perhaps half a lifetime, to write literature of enduring value, about one tenth of the present output!

## Too Much and Too Poor

In newspapers we have the most and I hope the worst in the world. I hope so, because I do hope no other country has anything as bad as our worst newspapers. We are said to consume 79 pounds of newsprint per capita, far more than any other country, mostly in newspapers, which devote 80 per cent to advertisement and perhaps 2 or 3 per cent to significant news, the rest to promotion of McCarthy and McCarthyism and to gossipy news of the sort that Americans seem to enjoy because it calls for no mental effort. Some time ago, I looked over and partly read almost all the first page of my Lawrence paper, a pretty good newspaper, then noticed that something in it seemed a bit familiar, looked at the heading, and saw that it was two days old. I had read it two days before—had wasted ten minutes on it for obviously I had remembered practically nothing. Too much newspaper!

Our schools are knee-deep in the overproduction business too. In our educational development, as the Beards once said: "Courses of instruction were divided and sub-divided, dissolving earlier philosophies of life and practice and multiplying academic goods almost as rapidly as inventors multiplied material commodities." Today the catalogue of an American university, or even of a college, is almost as big as a Sears Roebuck catalogue, a fantastically bloated list of fantastically specialized courses, not half of which are worth the time of a leisure-class mummy. Although teachers are better trained today than they used to be and standards of work are generally higher, a student had a better chance of getting a real education 50 years ago because the proportion of significant courses was greater. The responsibility for this proliferation of courses, by the way, lies largely with the faculties rather than with the administrative heads. Too much and too poor describes our academic provender.

So we of the middle and upper classes have too much and too poor of many things, and the evils of this are easy to see. In the first place, we have to work to turn out all this stuff at a sacrifice of our leisure time. Or, if we think our leisure is adequate or that we would not know what to do with more if we had it, we sacrifice important economic and aesthetic values. America is in many respects an ugly country with its slums—among the worst in the civilized world—its roadside junk yards, its eroded farms, its devastated forests, its unsightly houses in monotonously standardized and uninteresting towns. Instead of wasting our time producing stuff of little value could we not clean our country up, build more dams to utilize water power now wasted, build a few hundred hospitals, beautify our unlovely highways, study with more energy and resources some of our most dreaded diseases?

In the second place, grinding out standardized rubbish cannot be a satisfying or ennobling sort of activity. We could make some work less stultifying, more pleasant, if we produced fewer and better things. Workmen who produce cheap and trivial stuff can get little fundamental satisfaction in doing it. They only make a living. Consider the movies. What creative joy can men get in writing the scripts or the music for the dullest 90 per cent of our movies; what development of personality, what sense of achievement can the players get from acting in them? What joy in devoting God-given brains, if any, to writing the scripts of the radio soap operas, or trying to refurbish the thousands of jokes called for by the comedians, or drawing the cartoons for the comic strips? Imagine men made in the image of God writing the pornographic pulps sold in 25-cent editions (How many hundreds of millions are sold really?) or painting the billboards that line our highways! Such work as this, surely it must be painful, stultifying, degrading, a sort of prostitution quite as bad as that which we have made illegal. If workers could produce fewer and better products they would live nobler lives.

A third evil of our overproliferation of goods is that it forces on producers a gigantic task of selling. Whenever consumers are satisfied, the producers must call their puissant cohorts together and set them to the task of making the people dissatisfied and unhappy with what they have so that they will buy more goods. A satisfied people—let us say "groveling in contentment"—do not constitute a good market. Indeed this battle to make the people unsatisfied and unhappy and to make them work harder to earn more money so that they can buy something new so they can again be satisfied, goes on all the time; and its net result is that the people are unsatisfied much of the time. In this respect they may be in worse plight than they were long ago. Perhaps it may not be as bad to want a bicycle or a buggy as to want a new car and a new radio and a television set and a dish washer and a disposall and an airplane and a third bathroom and a trip to Europe. At any rate, selling is our most important activity, enrolling roughly half of the working population.

But suppose the products are good. Is it possible that there could be too much of any one thing or of most things, good quality assumed? To most Americans who measure life in quantitative terms the answer is clear: the more goods the richer the life—to the point where, if there were unlimited supplies of all goods, free, we should have Heaven. Our good people are a bit vague in their conception of Heaven, but in its broad outlines it would be a place where every member of the family has a Cadillac, a tiled bathroom, and a television set.

I wonder, however, whether there may not be too much of any one thing, or even of all. As Shakespeare, a very eminent writer, once said: "They are as sick that surfeit with too much, as they that starve with nothing." Most philosophers are at least agreed that happiness cannot be found in abundance of goods. Man is, after all, a simian; and the simian mind cannot have been designed for an infinite number of stimuli, for the solution of an infinite number of complexities. Man is probably happiest in a fairly simple environment, rich enough to provide health and a good life span, reasonable cleanliness and some beauty, but simple enough to be understood—one that does not present too many complexities and distractions. The scientific and technological advances have brought complications, not only in technology but in economic problems, to a point quite beyond the average man's understanding. My father lived without many luxuries we now think of as necessities, but he knew how to care for his modest possessions—a horse is simpler than a car, less often out of order and easier to start. He did not have to worry about the Korean or Indo-Chinese situation, or the problems of communism, atomic warfare or international diplomacy. Aside from his relatively poor health and short life he was probably as happy as we are today.

*Too Much and Too Poor*

There may well be too many of some things, even if good. For instance, we used to sing that lovely old Christmas song, *Stille Nacht, Heilige Nacht* a few times every Christmas season; and we loved it. Today I think we have a bit too much of it. Two weeks before Christmas the radio begins to bang out *Stille Nacht,* straight and with jazz variations. Along the bacchanalian pre-Christmas streets loudspeakers, with no regard for consistency, blare at every street corner *Stille Nacht* and *Joy to the World.* We hear *Stille Nacht* along with Bright Beer and Nutrena Chicken Feed until we may almost wish the damn thing had never been written except for the fact that if it weren't a clatter of *Stille Nacht* it would be something worse. I believe we can have too much of a good thing. If we're going to sing *Stille Nacht* I say let's have a little stille nacht instead of pandemonium.

Our plethora of goods—very shabby goods in the field of recreational and cultural activities—has not, I think, made us a particularly happy people. It always seemed to me that the Danes, French, and Swiss people are at least as happy as we are. Of course, most of them lack bathrooms, automobiles and television; but a troop of Danish bicyclers on their way into the country for a picnic is a cheery sight. John Dewey believed that even our business leaders do not have a very wonderful time: "One cannot look into the inner consciousness of his fellows; but if there is any degree of inner contentment on the part of those who form our pecuniary oligarchy, the evidence is sadly lacking. As for the many, they are impelled hither and yon by forces beyond their control." Of course they are active, busy, bustling, running about like frightened ants. They are trying to get more money so they can buy more things and so show that they are good Americans.

Americans seem to me to be a blasé and jaded people in some ways in spite of their physical activity and their Niagara of goods, irresponsive to the simpler and quieter forms of enjoyment, somewhat like the Romans in the time of Nero. On the highway, we drive not as if we wished to see the countryside but as if Cutty-Sark were after us to drag us down to hell. Our popular movies are often grand spectacles, some of them costing millions but perhaps quite lacking artistic merit; many of our radio dramas drip with the blood of from one to half a dozen victims—mostly beautiful blondes; but, of course, they always point the moral, "Crime does not pay," which for some reason no one is able to get across to the criminals.

In point of fatalities Nero did rather better in the Colosseum, but perhaps we shall be able to match him eventually. Like the Romans, we like great spectacles— we like to get into the largest crowds possible and yell, under organized direction. Some of our football crowds dwarf those of the Colosseum; but, of course, Nero never had any cheer leaders and the cheering must have been rather rowdy. In high schools and colleges only compulsory reading is customary; and athletics is crowding out other interests, it being less intellectual and more spectacular and therefore more appealing to Americans. The budget of a certain Kansas high school points the lesson: $3,500 for a coach and $25 for books; but this must have been an old-fashioned high school because even a fair-sized high school today should have about five or six coaches. Whether we shall see a time when schools will be devoted entirely to athletics we cannot predict, but certainly the field houses and gymnasiums make the libraries look like mausoleums, p o o r l y equipped and little used.

So we have too much and it's too poor, and we are busy producing and consuming it. One result of this and of our pecuniary measure of success is seen in the "externalization" of our lives. We are more anxious to *seem* than to *be*. We strive for baubles and gewgaws and gimcracks, good clothes and shiny cars rather than for contentment and fundamental culture. Another result, even more tragic, is that we can find no time or interest to learn much about the critical foreign and domestic problems, problems that we have heretofore been boggling and must solve if we are to maintain civilized life in America. Not only are we, in economics and politics, among the most unsophisticated yokels in the world, but we are precluded from solving our problems by the fact that we are so cocky and conceited because we have so many things. What other people have so many bathrooms and radios?

Our twentieth-century technology seems on the way to making the vast majority of our *people* surplus —just when the recent soaring birth rate promises more of this surplus. Two hundred able executives could and do manage the corporations that turn out more than half of our industrial goods; a score or two of great singers could entertain our people, fifty million at a time over the radio, and through the popular canning process could spread their entertainment throughout the day. A relatively few actors and actresses play the leading roles in our movies. A few hundred physical giants are all we need for our athletic teams. The spectators do yell patriotically to inspire the teams; but a few fire whistles, electric riveters and calliopes could make quite as much noise. A few thousand politicians are enough, and God knows they should be better; but if they were the people wouldn't elect them.

Of course, these few business leaders, entertainers and athletes should be good, should really be much better than they are or than, being human, they can possibly be. As for the rest of us, we make no difference one way or the other. We need just a few supermen. We need not blame the Creator of all men, good and bad, great and small, of course, but rather this infernal supertechnology we have built which does not fit the dimensions of human beings. The human beings, like most other things, are simply too many and too poor.

*. . . these spindle-legged, bowlegged, buck-kneed, stoop-shouldered devotees of unconventionality . . .*

# STUDENTS' SPINDLY SHANKS

*A letter written to the editor of the University Daily Kansan.*

Editor

University Daily Kansan:

May I call attention to a problem which seems to me to be of serious importance to the University. I refer to the undersize blue jeans that some of our more unconventional Bohemians are wearing on the campus.

I am not criticizing the jeans "per se," of course, for jeans show a democratic spirit, an indifference to external and superficial trappings and a deep interest in scholarly and spiritual values; I object to the size of the jeans—uniformly much too small and too tight. They reveal too much as to the generally poor architectural design of these young men.

We might overlook the fact that most men are decidedly spindle-legged, not built substantially like the football players, perhaps because pushing the accelerator does not develop the leg muscles as well as walking once did; but is there any reason why these fellows should make a display of their spider legs?

Even if the legs were straight, it would be an unnecessary revelation; but most of the spindles are not even decorously straight. Until recently I never realized how many bow-legged men there are in the University, perhaps the result of rickets or of the course in equitation.

As a matter of fact, most of these spindle legs are bent two ways at the knees, outward and forward—bow-legged and buck-kneed. The latter infirmity arises, no doubt, from the fact that the tight pants make it impossible to straighten the legs entirely. The possessor does have to bend his knees in sitting down and apparently is not able or does not dare to straighten them again.

One unfortunate result of this is that, unable either to straighten his legs or bend them much in walking, he slides his feet along shufflingly, like a communist on his way to a McCarthy inquisition. Another result of the tightness of his pants is that his feet look much too large, and often indeed are too large—swollen from interference with the circulation.

Furthermore, a buck-kneed man is usually stooped from a natural effort to complete the "S" figure and maintain a workable center of gravity and stable equilibrium. Tuberculosis naturally attacks such men.

Finally, I notice that these spindle-legged, bow-legged, buck-kneed, stoop-shouldered devotees of unconventionality habitually wear a look of anxiety. This is not because they haven't their lessons or are under indictment by the All-Student Council; it is because they are always wondering when a sudden vigorous movement may tear their skimpy swaddling from prow to stern, from belt to shoe tops.

Awaken, slaves of KU! You have only your pants to lose!

Surely something ought to be done about this. What is the All-Student Council for? Why does the Dean of Men ignore this problem? Roomier jeans would cost no more. Man is made in the image of God (can that really be true?); and he should not put his Maker and Model in an unfavorable light; just as I should think he would not want to betray his structural inadequacies to the ladies and destroy their illusions as to the "big strong mans."

Of course, the ladies wear jeans too, and their jeans seem tight and ill-adjusted, revealing—but that is outside the particular field of my professional competence.

Yours for more abundant jeans, for more efficient camouflage, for the fuller life, for life and legs untrammeled and unrestrained.

—John Ise

# THE MENACE OF COMMUNISM

*An address delivered before the Midwest Economics
Association.*

Hints of the communistic philosophy appeared very
early in the world's history, for such life forms as
the brachiopods, trilobites, crinoids, hydroids and radio-
laria were communistic in their habits. This is doubtless
the reason that they never developed high culture. We
have in the present world many such beings—oysters,
ants, and other insects, and even the higher simians—
which have similarly failed to develop culturally. The
lesson of geology and biology is clear to all who
will read.

It is not yet certain whether communism in man
is a natural and hereditary trait like red hair or hooked
noses or whether, like witchcraft, it is an acquired
characteristic. It has been observed that although some
communists appear to live in families, somewhat like
Presbyterians, there are apparently no baby communists; and it is not unusual to find in the same family,
and presumably of the same parentage, some children

who develop into communists and others who become Republicans. From such evidence it is sometimes assumed that communism is an acquired character, a result of some environmental abnormality; but we cannot be quite sure of this. Perhaps the genes of communism like those of genius or insanity may be generally dormant and may appear only sporadically. Or, perhaps mental and spiritual traits which are generally recognized as hereditary may make a child predisposed or susceptible to communism, somewhat as some children are susceptible to hay fever.

Much more might be learned if communists were not very difficult to study scientifically, owing to their habit of frequenting dark places and coming out only at night. There is some doubt as to many of their habits. Whether they are carnivorous and cannibalistic has not been authoritatively determined. Many students of communism believe that they are but that some are more fastidious than others. Some will apparently eat flesh raw while others prefer it roasted. It is asserted by Herkimer that they will not eat the flesh of other communists but only that of capitalists and aristocrats —perhaps because the proletarians, being hardened by physical work and exposure, are generally tough and lacking in flavor.

The many resemblances of communists to witches have impressed nearly all observers, although witches are not quite all alike or, at any rate, are variously described by those who have given most attention to the observation and recording of their habits and characteristics. Both communists and witches are generally conceded to be most active at night, but whether this is because of optical weakness or because of sensitiveness about their personal appearance is an unsettled question. Neither communists nor witches can be considered attractive by ordinary standards, and perhaps they are both somewhat conscious of the general public disapprobation of their appearance—just as anyone would be under similar conditions. Such characteristics are generally indicative of low social and pecuniary standing about which they could scarcely be otherwise than sensitive in clear daylight. Indeed, it is a definitely hopeful circumstance that witches and communists show this shame about their appearance for it indicates an appreciation of the importance of capitalist standards of reputability, and even perhaps a hope that these unfortunate beings may finally be induced to bestir themselves and try to improve their status.

In some other respects they differ considerably. It appears that communists are predominantly pedestrian in habits; but witches are often equestrian, so strongly so that they will ride broomsticks if nothing better is available and sometimes at very great speeds. In this respect witches are probably more dangerous than communists, although it would be easy to exaggerate the difference, for witches have been identified and studied for a much longer period than communists, and their vices are better known. In their general ideals and philosophy, communists are doubtless far more dangerous than witches. Witches usually attack only the persons of their victims, suck a little blood, or scratch an eye out, perhaps turn a luckless victim into a cat or a pig; but they do not, like communists, attack the Constitution and private property itself. Communists have seldom been known to poison wells, turn men into black cats, or vice versa; but they have no respect for private property. It is, of course, for this reason that they are regarded with greater abhorrence than witches and greater fear.

Witches seldom threaten our sacred institutions. The witches who counseled Macbeth did indeed lead him to commit murder and finally take Duncan's property; but perhaps they did not really mean to go so far, did not realize the lengths to which Macbeth's ambition might lead him. Certainly they should have been more careful in what they said. When witches do property damage, they usually do it not in the communist spirit of malicious hostility to the home, the church and private property but in a spirit of mischievousness. The witch, Cutty-Sark, which chased Tam O'Shanter across the river seemed not to want to claim him as husband but to burn him in hell; and it was only by inadvertence or awkwardness that she was guilty of the destruction of property in tearing his horse's tail nearly off. This did indeed mar the horse appreciably, not only in the matter of appearance and salability but in general utility, for a horse needs a tail to fight flies with. It was a cruel deed; yet, Cutty-Sark's motives were not communistically destructive for she was really reaching for Tam. The Lorelei, apparently a witch of compelling charm but evil disposition, one of the few historic witches credited with singing, was responsible for the destruction of much property along the Rhine; but she was apparently not moved by any philosophy hostile to the sacred right of private property but merely by a generally malicious spirit.

Communists are often hostile to church and to religion which they call the "opiate of the people"; but in this they show little understanding of the nature of

the present world and of the need of the people for
an opiate of some kind, particularly if it could be given
to Congress. Their ambition appears to be to destroy
the old bourgeoisie and aristocrats and to become a new
class of aristocrats themselves; but it is difficult to see
any gain in changing aristocrats since the ones we have
are accustomed to being aristocrats and can perform
their proper functions without strain; whereas, any new
class of aristocrats would have to work very hard in
that position.

From the very beginning, the Jews have been
leaders in the communist movement. Adam appears to
have had a definitely communistic society in the Garden of Eden, if we may judge from the circumstances
attending the famous apple episode. To the uninitiated,
this episode will not seem important; but to the trained
economist or historian it is pregnant with meaning. The
serpent did not *sell* Eve an apple, be it noted—the biblical record refers to it as "fruit"; but there is strong
evidence that it was an apple and probably a Ben Davis,
although Californians *insist* that it was a Sunkist orange.
He did not ask for any "quid pro quo," for any consideration, as he certainly would today in a capitalistic
economy. The serpent appears to have been impelled
by no acquisitive profit motive; he did not higgle and
bargain but gave her the apple freely. His motives
were not the highest, but at any rate he did not self-
ishly seek a profit. Apples were evidently very plentiful
in the Garden of Eden; and, of course, no one could
have made a profit dealing in free apples.

The fact that communism reigned in the Garden
of Eden should not be urged as an argument for communism, however, for the Garden was not a very attrac-

tive place in all ways, by present standards. There were indeed plenty of apples apparently; but there must have been something wrong with them; and even if they had been good, it would have been unpleasant to pick them in an orchard infested with snakes. It is probable that Eden lacked many other foods that we now enjoy in a capitalist society—hamburgers, bananas and mince pie, for instance. There is reason to believe that Adam and Eve chose their diet from a very restricted menu, one which may have lacked important vitamins. Since they did not have the radio, it is likely that they did not even understand their very great need for vitamins and laxatives and that their health was poor. Since there was no advertising, it is difficult to understand how they developed a want for clothes; but apparently the serpent and the apple had some significance in this matter. There is evidence of an awakening of the modern capitalistic spirit and process in the fact that Adam and Eve were *ashamed* of their lack of clothing quite as we are today, even when we have a few suits of old clothes to wear. Psychologists have often asserted that our shame in an inadequate supply of clothes is due to our splendid advertising service; but since Adam and Eve did not have the advantages of modern advertising, this is clearly an error. It appears rather that our shame in such matters is in accordance with long-established divine laws and that our modern advertisers are merely implementing and applying those laws.

Neither can we see in the story of the Garden of Eden any support for the communist argument that it is capitalism that has destroyed the natural goodness of man. Neither historians nor psychologists have made a careful analysis of Adam's character so we do not know much about him; but it is clear that his character was in process of being undermined before he left the Garden of Eden. Such evidence as we have suggests that men have lost their original virtues, if any, not through the influence of capitalism and the institution of private property but through association with women.

Later Hebrews established private property in cattle and asses and men servants and women servants and gold and silver and land and wives; and Jacob's strategy in securing Esau's birthright was as definitely capitalistic in spirit as was Jay Gould's later strategy in acquiring railroads. The worship of the golden calf by the Israelites under Aaron is probably symbolic of the mores of capitalism, perhaps prophetic of the gold standard or of the gold hoard now held by the government in Kentucky. There is, on the other hand, much evidence that communistic influences were at work in ancient Judea as in present-day America. It is recorded that the wrath of the Lord waxed hot against the Israelites for worshipping the golden calf; but probably this should be regarded as communistic propaganda against the capitalistic system. Certainly David's liaison with Bathsheba suggests a trend toward modern communistic free love.

Communistic infection of the ancient H e b r e w prophets is indicated by their general hostility to money lending. The Mosaic law prohibited "usury of money, usury of victuals, usury of anything that is lent upon usury"—usury, of course, meaning interest. Perhaps it is fortunate that Christian capitalistic nations have not followed the rules laid down in the Old Testament. Certainly such great financial leaders as Stephen Girard, Russell Sage and Hetty Green would have been gravely handicapped had the biblical prohibition of usury been in force in Christian America.

It is often claimed by communists that their wicked and subversive doctrines are not altogether unlike the precepts of the Christian religion. They see significance in the fact that Jesus was a proletarian, a man of the lower classes, born in a manger, later a carpenter, a member of the working class although not of a union; in the fact that his father, or perhaps we should say the husband of his mother, although a descendant of the House of David, was apparently a man of little wealth and dignity; and in the fact that Mary herself spoke of her "low estate" and did not complain of it but merely mentions it as a circumstance, apparently not dissatisfied or ambitious to better herself—perhaps because there were no enterprising advertisers in Galilee.

The communists see significance too in the fact that Jesus associated much with the poor, indeed, seems to have preferred to associate with the lower classes and to have been particularly solicitous of their welfare while, like Roosevelt, He heaped aspersions on the rich. They point out, too, the fact that when Jesus distributed the loaves and fishes he charged nothing for them but gave them freely—a clear precedent, it must be conceded, for the activities of the AAA, the WPA, the Relief Administration and the Surplus Commodities Corporation. This, of course, tended to reduce the profits of retailers and to abate the confidence of the businessmen of Galilee where there was no efficient chamber of commerce to guard against such contingencies; and this attack on the capitalist system has never received from historians the attention that it merits. Yet, without further historical research, we are safe in assuming that the distribution of the loaves and fishes was not communistic in its purpose. This must also be said of the driving of the money changers out of the temple and of the reference to the temple as a den of thieves, which have often been cited as precedents for New Deal criticism of bankers. Whether this was the precedent for the Pecora investigation of New York bankers has not been established conclusively, but at any rate Jesus and Pecora appear to have come to somewhat similar conclusions regarding the banking business. It is unfortunate that Jesus could not have been as charitable with the money changers as with the fallen woman and the thieves on the cross.

It must be confessed that on various occasions Jesus expressed a gravely critical attitude toward the profit motive. It was the Devil, let us note, who took Him up on the mountain and offered Him all the kingdoms of the world; and the fact that Jesus refused indicates clearly that He recognized His tempter and that He did not approve of the general motive which leads to the acquisition of large properties. Perhaps, in refusing the Devil's offer of the whole world, He did not intend to throw into unfavorable light the later careers of such great capitalist leaders as Cecil Rhodes, Vanderbilt and Rockefeller; yet, inevitably, His action has often been so interpreted. Such an interpretation may seem justified in the light of various other declarations of Jesus against covetousness reported by Saint Luke—for instance, "Take heed, and beware of covetousness"—and that He regarded the accumulation of wealth as un-Christian. His clear statement that a rich man can hardly enter into the Kingdom of Heaven leaves no room for doubt on that point; and this declaration, to-

gether with Karl Marx's contention that there is no
proper place for the rich on earth, leaves only one
place in which the rich can be said to have appropriate
surroundings.

It is true that Jesus did not conceive the Marxian
strategy of shooting the great capitalists. He only said
that they could not go to Heaven which, by implication,
meant that they would be entertained elsewhere; and
thus, perhaps without intending it, Jesus formulated the
great principle which governs the apportionment of
rewards among Christian capitalist peoples. The rich
get theirs on earth, and the poor get theirs in Heaven.
This has been satisfactory to so many people and for
so long a time that we must view with the deepest abhorrence the activities of those communists who would
undermine the faith of the poor in their future of infinite
rewards. When the poor have lost their confidence in
the future, they begin insistently to clamor for more
of the scarce goods of earth; and the New Deal is the
tragic result—with communism looming as a final
possibility.

It is indeed very difficult to reconcile all this with
the moral development of Christian capitalist peoples.
The covetousness motive appears to have been the great
moving force behind all economic and moral progress,
the great, creative urge impelling men to serve their
fellow men by serving themselves first. Without it,
how would it have been possible to finance the splendid
churches in which our peoples meet together every
Sunday to hear the messages about the dangers of covetousness; how would it be possible to pay the preachers
and the organists and the choirs and the janitors and
the cooks and the grocerymen? In all fine churches

there are rich and covetous men who help to pay these expenses, no doubt hoping that Jesus was too pessimistic as to their future.

It is all quite puzzling, but perhaps it is not necessary that we should understand it fully. Certainly in interpreting Jesus' criticisms of rich businessmen, it would be unfair to assume that they would be equally applicable to the businessmen of today, to businessmen who have been refined and ennobled by luncheon clubs, chambers of commerce, trade associations, athletic clubs, business schools, to men whose moral standards have been propped up on the leaning side by the restrictive codes of New Deal agencies. We must not ignore the great moral development of businessmen in the past 2,000 years.

So we repudiate all communist claim to Christian principles or affinity with Christian principles. We must repudiate, too, the communist argument that in their doctrine of the class struggle they are merely following the precedent set by Jesus in his criticisms of the rich and in his sympathy with the poor. Capitalism thrives best where the people are one happy family, all with identical interests. This does not mean that the interests of the rich are the same as those of the poor but rather that the interests of the poor are the same as those of the rich; or as Herbert Hoover has so clearly pointed out that whatever is good for the rich is good also for the poor and, therefore, that the people are really one happy family and that those who stress the difference between rich and poor are destroying the harmony in the family and undermining capitalism.

Other views held by Jesus are ill-fitted to guide men in a capitalist society. He never saw the true moral value of thrift and industry; and, no doubt, His teachings had much to do with the development of shiftlessness under the New Deal. "Behold the fowls of the air: for they sow not, neither do they reap, nor gather into barns." "Consider the lilies of the field, how they grow; they toil not, neither do they spin." "Take therefore no thought for the morrow; for the morrow shall take thought for the things of itself." Such precepts, although not clearly communistic, seem calculated to undermine the qualities of thrift, foresight and self-reliance upon which capitalism depends and, therefore, to bring the conditions out of which communism may be expected to develop. Those who plan their carefree lives after those of the fowls of the air or the lilies of the field are always likely to come finally on the county; and those who lay not up for themselves any treasures upon the earth are sometimes obliged to rely upon the public treasury. Under the New Deal "everyone that asketh receiveth" which proves that the New Deal represents in some respects merely an attempt to apply Christian doctrines to some of the problems of government; but it is not certain that our capitalism will stand the strain indefinitely.

It must be conceded that our churches are a major factor in the spread of communism, for the churches are in many respects run on a communistic plan. Notwithstanding the fact that there is a considerable expense involved in the operation of a church, some preachers proclaim that salvation is free and charge no admission to their services. It is true that they always pass the collection plate around, but the poor need not contribute at all if they cannot do so or do not wish to. In many churches, no distinctions are drawn between the rich and poor, and all—that is, all people of the same color —are permitted to choose their own seats without restriction as to wealth or social position. All are permitted to enjoy the same sermon, the same music, under the same conditions in all respects; and often the preacher shakes hands with all as they leave the church. In some churches, the various members, without respect to wealth or social position, are requested and permitted to offer extemporaneous prayers; and the members sometimes address each other and the preacher as "brothers" and "sisters," somewhat as communists call each other "comrades." In such churches, we have what is practically a Marxian classless society. Those who wish to protect American institutions from subversive influences may well give this matter their earnest attention.

It is very unfortunate that this manner of conducting church services often forces the preachers into a hypocritical position which doubtless causes them much embarrassment. Schooled in Christian doctrines, they must assume that the rich cannot go to Heaven; yet, also devoted to the upbuilding of their churches, they must accept the contributions of the rich; and in doing so, they must hold out to them a hope which can only prove illusory. In the law this is known as getting money under false pretenses, a very grave offense for all but preachers. Mind you, I do not say this in any spirit of caviling or censure for I feel deeply the tragedy of the preachers' dilemma; and there are mitigating circumstances. The preachers do not get the money for themselves, but for the cause of spreading the teachings of Jesus—or, at any rate, those parts of the teachings which do not refer to rich men, covetousness, and the like. Their motives are not selfish, not even capitalistic. Furthermore, contributions by the rich may at least lessen the moral turpitude involved in being rich and mitigate the rigors of the punishment later to be meted out to them. If we may trust the reports of Dante, there are several circles of purgatory with differing forms of punishment provided to fit various grades of iniquity; and perhaps by contributing to the church, the rich may at least raise their standing in hell. Perhaps this is the reasoning by which the preachers justify the acceptance of the money of the rich. It is obvious, too, that the rich are less rich by the amount of their contributions and, therefore, in better moral position—which the preachers may rightly urge as an argument for heavy contributions. Yet it seems unjust that our great business leaders must thus choose between giving their money away in this world and roasting in the next.

Doubtless there is some encouragement to communism also in the pictures of Heaven drawn by some of our church leaders. Heaven is pictured as an area within which all are equally rich because there is abundance of all good things—that is, all goods are free goods as economists would say; and, therefore, there is no basis for inequality because only the poor of earth can enter here. Since there is plenty, there is, of course, no need for the institution of private property. Here is the Marxian classless society again although the bourgeoisie are eliminated in a somewhat different way than Marx envisaged and in a manner not altogether unsatisfactory since purgatory represents the businessman's ideals better than Heaven. Here in purgatory there is a healthy scarcity and a possibility of trafficking a bit in water and ointments and special favors from the Devil, who is said to be profit-minded and not above such things. While the bourgeoisie presumably lack the vulgar physical comforts they once enjoyed they probably have some of the conditions that gave life its high spiritual zest and meaning on earth.

Unfortunately, we have other institutions in which the principles of organization and management are more or less communistic. Our public schools are supported by the government; the teachers are hired by the government; and the children of all classes are given the same training in all respects without payment of any kind. The pupils sit in seats assigned without regard to the wealth or quality of their parents and are supposed to receive the same treatment. Occasionally teachers do indeed find it necessary to show proper consideration for the children of bankers and lumbermen and for the children of members of the school board, but such special consideration is contrary to the general communistic rule governing the schools. The same general situation is found in state colleges and universities where not only are the students of all social classes taught by the same teachers in the same rooms and all together at the same time but many live in fraternity houses or communistic barracks where there is complete common ownership of all furnishings. Here is Plato's Republic in all its sinister outlines.

Is it any cause for wonder that so many of our teachers and students are communists when they live thus in communistic surroundings much of every day? It is true that they are often at home in the mornings and evenings; and they usually sleep at home; but in the home there are communistic influences at work too.

All members of the family use the same bathroom, eat the same food at the same table, perhaps drive the same car, read the same books and papers, listen to the same radio; father and sons often wear the same shirts and socks, smoke the same brand of cigarettes from the same humidor sitting before the same fireplace. Here we have the Marxian classless society or, indeed, even worse, for rewards are here inversely related to productivity and merit. Babies lie around in the shade most of the time, awakening just often enough to cry for food and attention; yet they usually receive the most generous consideration; children play most of the time; yet they share fully in the family income while the parents who do the work must content themselves with whatever is left after the baby and the children have been provided for. This is the home, mark you, that misguided sentimentalists have all too often referred to as the incubator of sterling American character. It is high time that the protectors of American institutions look into the schools and homes of our land.

In yet other institutions we find the same encroachment of communistic principles: in libraries, museums, hospitals, parks, streets and highways, jails and insane asylums. The number of these increases with every passing year. We have in the United States 165,000,000 acres of forest lands communistically owned like the forests of Russia; we have a score of national parks in which no private capitalism is permitted, where millions of American citizens seek recreation every summer exposed constantly to the insidious spirit of Karl Marx. In such societies as the Rotary and Kiwanis Clubs, the members at their meetings forget all class distinctions, eat together, and greet each other in the same brotherly and informal manner that communists use at their secret meetings. Many of the great fraternal orders—the Elks, Moose, Eagles, Woodmen, and Masons—are so similar to communist locals that it is difficult to see how they have so long escaped the watchful eye of the McCarthy Committee. Like the communists, the members of such orders usually meet at night in secret sessions; like the communists, they speak of their members as brothers of whom all are equal within the order and in the sight of the Lord; like the communists they demand secrecy and undivided loyalty; like the communists they have no general wide differentiation in money rewards but depend upon honors and prestige to inspire the members to work for the good of the orders. Just as Malenkov receives only $150 a month, the highest Potentates and Wizards and Kleagles receive only modest salaries for their services, or perhaps none at all. Since the meetings of these orders are secret, it is not known that there are any subversive activities at their meetings; but they should doubtless be investigated. Certainly that classic of American brotherhood, sung at all their festivities, is ill-fitted to foster individualism—*The More We Get Together the Happier We'll Be*. Clearly, the more we get together the more communistic we'll be.

The McCarthy Committee and the Jenner Committee and the Velde Committee have pointed out that there are many communists in the government service; but these vigilant guardians have not fully apprehended the seriousness of this situation. Let us not evade the issue. Our government, like all governments to the extent of its activities, is and must be essentially communistic in character. Communism means government ownership of all goods and government operation of all enterprises; and to the extent that we expand the services of government, we approach the communistic ideal. The government employees at Washington do not own their offices and office equipment; they do not work for their own gain but for the general good or harm of all.

In this connection, we can see that the American people themselves are more gravely tainted with the virus of communism than even our stanchest patriots have realized. When President Harding and Secretary Fall tried to turn the oil reserves from government control to private development—from communism to capitalism—our leading statesmen and many of the people themselves promptly denounced these men for their patriotic efforts. Albert Fall had apparently received a monetary consideration for his efforts as was proper and necessary in a capitalist society; and the oil men, also guided by the profit motive, were ready to proceed with the development of these reserves in the American way. Yet the American people themselves, unable to see the true significance of this, demanded that the reserves be returned to communistic government control. If some patriotic American citizen were to steal the White House and turn it into a private office building, very likely many people would insist that it be returned to the government, perhaps all the while mouthing denunciations of communism. Unless the people can be educated to see the significance of government policies, there can be little hope for American capitalism.

It is cheering to all that recently the Americans have developed more patriotic and capitalistic attitudes in such matters. When President Eisenhower, in his valiant effort to balance the budget, gave away federal oil lands, the people were very happy about it. It is true that the President had received no money for the oil as he should have under true capitalism, but he got the votes of several states which had a definite cash value in later government activities.

We would feel fairly secure if the guardians of American peace and safety—the Army and Navy—could be relied upon to offer a solid front against the encroachments of communism. Unfortunately, however, there are strongly communistic elements in the Army and Navy. Both are government agencies and, therefore, inclined to a favorable view of government activities. In both, many of the lower classes of the employed live in government barracks where little private ownership is permitted. Even the guns and sabres are the property of the government. If these soldiers and sailors kill soldiers and sailors of the enemy forces, they make no extra profit by their valor but receive only their regular wages; and if they kill no one, their wages are paid just the same. Even Lenin was obliged to abandon the principle of equal wages for all in order to stimulate industry and energy in the workers, and the Army and Navy may well consider the advantages of this. Perhaps a payment of a certain reward for each enemy scalp would provide a proper capitalist incentive for military efficiency.

How have so many communistic practices and institutions percolated into the fabric of American society? What insidious forces have been at work to bring us to this condition of communistic infection in our churches, our schools and homes, our brotherly orders, our government, our Army and Navy? We have already seen that the communistic tradition goes far back to the time of the ancestral orangoutangs and that it appeared sporadically throughout antiquity. At its very birth the American Government started with the definite suggestion of communism in its birth certificate for among the "self-evident truths" in the *Declaration of Independence* were the statements that "all men are created equal" and that whenever any form of government becomes destructive of the ends for which it was designed the people have a right "to alter or to abolish it, and to institute new Government . . . in such form . . . most likely to effect their safety and happiness." These statements are made without equivocation, mind you, in a document which was presented to the people of all classes as a rallying cry for a revolutionary war, a document which immature children of the time and of later times were permitted to read. It was heartening to the lower classes, of course, to be told that all men were equal; but the implications of that statement point directly to the Marxian classless society as the ideal form of government, while the statement that the people have a right to change their form of government is an invitation to communistic propaganda and violence which patriotic persons today, and I gravely fear too late, are striving to suppress. All this was written, too, by men who were at the time plotting to overthrow the established government and seize power for themselves, by men who later confiscated much of the property of the governors. Is it too much to say that the *Declaration of Independence* should be withheld from the general public, particularly from young and immature minds, along with Karl Marx's *Capital?* It is true that the *Declaration* set up as inalienable certain capitalist rights, including, as Professor Davies once expressed it, "the right to Life, Liberty, and the Pursuit of Property"; but the writers of that document did not see how difficult that pursuit would be in a later era.

This is not all. In our American histories, many of them studied in our schools by young and impressionable children, are eulogistic stories of Washington, Jefferson, Franklin, Patrick Henry—all of them *revolutionists*, conspiring and fighting against the established government. Is it to such men that our children must look for inspiration in their lives? How shall we make clear to our children the reasons for electing Washington president and hanging John Brown? How can we instill in their minds and souls the virtues of obedience, loyalty and respect for government when their historic idols are revolutionists who rose to their historic stature by overthrowing the established government? These were honorable men, no doubt, in their way; perhaps they were misled by the alien philosophies of European revolutionaries; but their revolutionary activities cannot be condoned.

It seems a paradoxical circumstance that some of our most reputable people, wives and daughters of honorable and distinguished citizens, should feel no shame in their genealogical descent from these early revolutionists but should even take pride in such an ancestry. I have only respect and affection for the Daughters of the First American Revolution. They cannot justly be held accountable for the deeds of forbears over whom they could have had no control. This august and noble sisterhood have themselves lived exemplary lives of devotion to our American ideals which should raze from our memories the unfortunate deeds of their ancestors; and they merit the plaudits of a grateful people for their earnest and untiring efforts to guard American institutions from subversion. Yet, as long as they themselves proudly flaunt in their very name the word which has been the rallying cry of communism, their efforts cannot be as effective as we might wish.

But the Daughters of the First American Revolution are not the only ones of ancient lineage whose example offers a threat to American institutions. There are tribes of Indians in the Southwest, Indians whose families are older and more distinguished than the Revolutionary Fathers, who live in pueblos in a state closely approximating communism; and many tourists go out there to see them, perhaps taking immature children along with them. Yet the McCarthy Committee has taken no note of this situation at all. At one time there were many more of these communistic Indians in the cliffs of Colorado, Arizona, New Mexico and Utah. Because of their communistic organization, many of them have perished, leaving only their empty stone dwellings as a tragic warning of the danger of alien philosophies; yet there are many such communities still in operation in flagrant violation of capitalist principles.

The extent to which the American people have been infected with the communist spirit is clearly shown in some recent elections. The New Deal is well known to have been inspired by the communist labor unions; yet when the polls indicated that the lower classes wanted the New Deal, all our statesmen promised the people more communistic New Deal. Such valiant defenders of the American Way as Thomasius Stentorius Dewey and Jonathan Americanus Bricker did constantly inveigh against all things communistic, or things resembling or related to or neighboring with or tending toward or similar to or insufficiently dissimilar to communism, yet to no avail. The supernumerary submarginal suckers of the social substratum did thirst for the communistic New Deal as the hart panteth for the water brooks; and these valiant knights of rugged individualism, free enterprise and the American Way were constrained to offer them even more New Deal than the communistic New Dealers had offered. The election became a contest in the expansion and elaboration of the New Deal, in plagiarizing *Das Kapital,* in undermining the spirit of free American enterprise which all did so greatly love and cherish; and all of this proves that American democracy moves in mysterious ways its wondrous blunders to perform.

These are the times that try men's souls. We must devote our energies unselfishly to the problem of reversing the present drift toward communism; but the measures appropriate to this end are not easy to devise. How, for instance, shall we change the communistic home or lessen the happiness that the untutored masses find in the home? We cannot, of course, eliminate the home. Without it, where would we put mother, where would great men be born, over what would the vines grow? Without the home, we should have no home on the range. Clearly we cannot eliminate the communistic home. But we might make it less attractive by continuance of food and fuel rationing or perhaps by requiring every family to keep a few cows for the children to milk.

As to the Church, it is doubtful if we could persuade the church trustees to charge a suitable fee for the services. Even if we could persuade the preachers to stress the story of the talents and the story of Jacob and Esau more heavily and the condemnation of covetousness and the damnation of the rich less heavily, we should only have scratched the bark of our problem. We can scarcely dismantle our communistic libraries, museums, hospitals, jails, parks and insane asylums as long as the lower classes are permitted to vote on government policies; we scarcely even dare to break up our communistic college fraternities.

The seriousness of our situation calls for immediate revising of our so-called educational system, for the elimination of the studies which foster a communistic spirit in our youth. Professor Goodwin Watson has shown that the radical spirit increases steadily with years in school; that, strange and tragic as it may seem, there is a close correlation between education and radicalism. At first superficial blush, it might appear that if we could abolish our schools we would strike at the roots of our problem, but such drastic action would bring a few serious difficulties. Where would our great industrial leaders get the engineers, scientists, lawyers, accountants, statisticians and salesmen for their businesses? Where would they get the journalists and advertisers to inform the masses about the virtues of free enterprise, rugged individualism, liver pills and vitamin tablets? The medieval churchmen saw the dangerous possibilities of general public reading; yet, if they had not learned to read the newspapers, how would the common workers be able to learn about the blessings of free enterprise and the dangers of communism, how would they make out their income taxes? And if the masses knew not arithmetic, how would they compute their surtax net incomes or their grocery bills?

How, without arithmetic, could we train the scientists and engineers needed by our great businessmen? Clearly the people must know arithmetic; and they must be able to read; and perhaps writing is not a serious evil although if Karl Marx had not been able to write there would have been no *Das Kapital* and no communism. Writing may be an innocent diversion, but it may be very destructive.

No, we cannot eliminate education entirely. It is essential to the profits of industry, and some of it does no harm. The study of arithmetic, even of higher arithmetic, and of chemistry, physics and engineering does not necessarily foster radicalism. The biological sciences are not equally innocent. In entomology and zoology, professors and students study the habits and customs of insects and animals which are almost purely communistic in habits—bees, ants, wasps, termites, beavers and many varieties of monkeys, the latter collaterally related to man himself. Even in botany, we find many species of plants which, perhaps for mutual protection, tend to grow in quasi-communistic patches.

It is another group of studies, however, which is largely responsible for the growth of communism in our schools, the so-called social sciences: history, sociology, political science, economics and psychology. Here is our main area of infection, the area from which spreads the canker of radicalism throughout the educational system. Here are the studies that make communists of our teachers and students. It has often been observed that the radicalism of students is in direct proportion to their knowledge of these studies; yet, some of these studies are offered to immature children in the grade and high schools. History is taught in almost all high schools. Quite truly it is taught in such a way as to mitigate its subversive effects as much as possible. Most of the attention is given to such matters as Washington and the cherry tree, but subversive ideas are smuggled into the study even of these episodes. Some historians, whether with communistic design or not I cannot say, have even raised questions as to the truth of the story of the cherry tree. Surely such teaching cannot strengthen the patriotism of our young people or deepen their devotion to the American system of free enterprise.

In our colleges, even worse conditions are not uncommonly found. Many professors in the social sciences inculcate in their students a critical and questioning attitude of mind which sometimes blossoms into radicalism. It is well known that it is the men of unquestioning loyalty and fidelity and optimism, the "boosters," who have made America what it is, or whatever it is; yet, here are professors, themselves crabbed critics, perhaps even pessimists, working persistently to undermine the innocence and optimism natural to youth and to raise in their places a spirit of doubt and uncertainty, of questioning, of criticism, perhaps a feeling of pessimism and unhappiness. Some of these professors have tried to develop in their students a *habit of thinking* even about the most important and controversial questions, apparently unconscious of or indifferent to the fact that once this habit is developed, there is no way of controlling the conclusions to which the students may finally come. Such professors do not see that they are thus setting in operation forces whose final fruits are utterly unpredictable. So we have economists raising questions about the motives and practices of such great and good men as Jay Gould and John D. Rockefeller, stressing class differences, perhaps questioning the happy family theory of American society and the percolation theory of prosperity and voicing approval of labor unions. It is even reported that some professors are members of labor unions.

Unfortunately, communistic influences are not confined to these social science studies. English and language departments of many colleges include a great many radicals—New Dealers, liberals, socialists, and communists. The reason for this is not definitely known; but since grammar and rhetoric appear not to be subversive in effect, the responsibility probably lies with the reading of literature. Here we see the danger of a general habit of reading. Not all literature is thus incendiary and subversive. If the study of literature could be restricted to Homer, Virgil, Longfellow, Dickens, Adam Smith and Westbrook Pegler, surely no harm would result; but there is always danger that people who can read may read such writers as Aristophanes, Juvenal, Voltaire, Mark Twain, Steinbeck and Drew Pearson. Indeed, so grossly have the public morals been perverted or so perverted are the people by nature, perhaps as a result of the apple episode of long ago, that many of them, particularly the young and immature, actually prefer the latter type of literature. If we can not prevent the people from reading, we must at least see that they do not read literature which undermines their faith in American institutions.

Indeed we must go much further. We must have a great cleansing conflagration, a burning of the books, a combustion of most of the so-called realistic and modernistic books of our decadent period, perhaps under the auspices of the Boston Watch and Ward Society and the Regents of the University of Texas. I hope I will not be charged with a pyromaniac disposition or with lack of patriotic enthusiasm or appropriate war hatred when I say that our sometime enemy, the Great Fuehrer, pointed the way we must go not only in burning subversive books but in taking a militant stand against all forms of communism. Having struck him down, we can do no better than to seize the torch that he so valiantly carried.

A ray of light illuminates the landscape. Already our statesmen at Washington have sensed the need of a more vigilant policy. It is cheering to see them establishing more and more patriotic detective and protective un-American committees. Now we can sleep in our sacred homes in peace and safety, undisturbed by communists and rumors of communists; now we may feel assured of the security and sanctity of our property if we have any property; now we shall see the American ship of state plowing the broad seas of free enterprise in the American Way with the whistle tied down and the ship gongs sounding a potpourri of *Star Spangled Banner, Horst Wessel* and *The More We Get Together the Happier We'll Be*. Double-distilled patriots who felt pangs of regret in destroying the Gestapos in Hitler's Fatherland can find comfort in the re-establishment of American Gestapos in the homeland of the brave and free.

For our un-American committees have established the principle which must guide American statecraft, the principle which brought such splendor to German culture under the leadership of the Great Fuehrer, the great *principle of unity and homogeneity*. This principle enunciates the one simple and eternal truth that the greatness of a nation and its people depends on the unity and homogeneity of its thought—its *Gleichanschauung*. All people must think alike and act alike. Communistic labor unions must be suppressed because they foster trends of thought and action which are different from those of the employers; liberals, socialists, radicals and other communists must be liquidated because they represent a dissenting minority, a fatal obstacle to national unity. Particularly important is it that such dissenters should be purged from government agencies and college faculties. Teachers present one of our most serious problems for they are not well homogenized, and some of them cling tenaciously to their individualistic propensities. Many of them are correct and impeccable Republicans, but some are New Dealers, pinks, leftists, progressives, Baptists, or even Socialists. Because of their tendency to individualistic deviationism, teachers have often been viewed with suspicion by our homochromatic citizens, yet they could not be eliminated because we could not have athletics without schools and it was assumed that we could not have schools without teachers. It is clear, however, that the teachers will have to be liquidated and a new kind of teachers given the task of training our youth, teachers who have not been exposed to education. We could find in the military the men and women who are ideally qualified to develop intellectual homogeneity in our schools.

Laborers would also present perplexing problems, for some of them are New Dealers and liberals; and we dare not liquidate them because they are needed in war and in industrial production. Joseph Stalin seems to have perfected ways of ironing out differences among laborers by liquidating those who hold incorrect views, and perhaps we should study his methods carefully; indeed we are already using some of his tactics with some success. Businessmen present a cheering picture of straight-line, undeviating conformity. They can usually be counted on to support the un-American committees that strive so nobly and pertinaciously to implement the great principle of Happiness Through Homogeneity.

Most unfortunately, we no longer have as the supreme head of the anti-communist and anti-witch forces of the world the great Fuehrer, Adolph Schickelgruber; but we have many valiant leaders in Congress and in other positions of power and behind them an army of patriotic citizens with arms and cymbals and drums and megaphones and poisoned stilettos—a militant host, ready to do battle for American unity, harmony, homogeneity and imbecility. *Heil und Vorwärts* be our battle cry! *Horst Wessel* be our song! Our goal, it doesn't matter, as long as we're on our way.

*. . . listening to the somnolent hum of the professor's voice.*

# THE LECTURE SYSTEM

*An address delivered before the Midwest Economics Association.*

Among the manifold blessings enjoyed by economists and by teachers generally, without doubt the most important, is the lecture system. Few of the men and women who live the rich, full life of the professor realize how much of their happiness is due to the high privilege of lecturing to classes of people who are required to sit attentively or perhaps even to listen respectfully. The desire to talk is one of the most common of all human aspirations, one which men in most callings are able to indulge only occasionally and intermittently, perhaps even at some expense—as, for instance, at social gatherings—and never for any considerable time or without interruption, for in any conversation all parties wish to wedge in a word here and there—to share in the joy of talking. No one can have a clear field; and if anyone indulges his natural "propensity to talk" at too great length, he may see his audience melting away. The professor is here supremely fortunate. He enjoys the privilege of in-

dulging to a practically unlimited extent the most insistent yearning of the human spirit, is paid for it, and is
sure of an audience. He has a system of examinations
and grades by which he can command the attention of
his audience, however superficial their interest, however
inept he may be in holding it. The students must have
degrees, to secure degrees they must have grades, to
acquire grades they must take examinations, and to pass
examinations they must listen to the lectures or read
the notes of others who have listened. It would be difficult to picture a happier situation.

The professor of economics does more than talk to
his classes—he *lectures*. His position is far more dignified than that of a mere conversationalist. Like the
prophet and oracle, he looks into the future and deci-
phers the forms of things to come; like the priest, he for-
mulates rules, codes and commandments by which society shall be saved; like the judge, he decides questions of
equity and expediency; like Moses, he speaks from the
mountain tops of truth and wisdom to his followers in
the valley of doubt; like God, he creates children in his
own (intellectual) image and then complains of their
manifold sins. It is satisfying to be in a position of so
much prestige and authority, even for only an hour; and
it is fortunate that professors can enjoy this since few of
them are in a position to enjoy the low but obvious distinction of pecuniary reputability.

It is to the lecture system that we must attribute the
fine personality so characteristic of professors. Philosophers often speak of the development of personality as
the highest aim of life; and through his activity as a lec-
turer, the professor achieves this development in su-

preme degree. Speaking oracularly to his followers, he develops poise and confidence; speaking much, he develops fluency and clarity of utterance; speaking from well-ordered and seasoned notes, he develops the habit of logical analysis and organization; discussing always matters of great importance, he develops power and precision of thought. Along with all this, he has his lighter moments in which he brightens up the discussion with shafts of wit and humor and with well-chosen and well-tested stories and so rounds out a full, happy and balanced personality which commands the affection as well as the respectful admiration of his students. Many students remember the personality of their instructors even after they have forgotten their lectures.

A further advantage of the lecture system is that it is not very hard work for the professor. With well-organized notes before him, he can pursue his subject at a minimum of mental strain and so reserve his fresh energies for research, for work on committees and for essential social and civic activities. By lecturing, he also avoids the disturbing effect of questions from the students. It is true that most students do not ask many questions. The better class of students particularly, trained and refined in the fraternities, do not ask questions either because they can think of none to ask, or because they recognize that evidence of interest in class is the unmistakable sign of the roughneck. Yet there are always a few students, unacquainted with the better social traditions, who may ask questions if the professor permits it and are likely to disturb the smooth flow of the professor's thought. The lecture system, of course, precludes such irregularities.

Through his practice in the classroom, the professor is competent also to lecture to other groups outside the academic circles, thus expanding and enlarging his influence over a wide area. He lectures to the Y.W.C.A. and the Y.M.C.A., church groups and home missions, societies for the promotion of prohibition, women's clubs and men's clubs, home study societies, farm organizations, veterans' and patriotic societies, and at high school graduation ceremonies. If there were no lecturing professors, the Rotary and Kiwanis clubs would soon cease to function; and the number of banquets would be greatly curtailed. We may well say that the lecture system of our universities is thus responsible for much of the best in American life.

There are some educators who insist that the professor should have his lectures printed and hand them out to the class to be read and that the students could learn better through reading than through listening to lectures. A Harvard study of this question some years ago indicated that the students learned twice as much from printed material as from lectures. It is clear however, that such procedure would have an unfortunate effect on the development of the professor's personality and, on the other hand, would deprive the students of the rich benefits of more personal association with their teacher. A university conducted on such a plan would be a dead, soulless institution, quite incapable of attracting young men and women seeking to develop their own personalities. Perhaps even worse, such a pedagogical method would greatly reduce the output of ideals, for in lecturing the professor can enunciate his ideas as fast as they come to him; whereas, if he were obliged to wait for the printing press, he would be greatly retarded and might even find some of his ideas quite out of date before they appeared in print. Students, particularly in the fast-changing science of economics, want fresh, up-to-date material which the professor can give only through lectures.

But there would be a further difficulty with the printing of the lectures. Speaking from his notes, the professor has a well-recognized function which perhaps justifies him in signing the pay roll. A good set of notes may serve thus for many years. The professor with such notes is in a position not altogether unlike that of the priest with his hand-written Bible before the days of printing—in a position of monopoly control of the means of salvation. If he were to print and scatter his ideas broadcast, he would have lost his enviable position, and perhaps even his excuse for existence—or at any rate, for signing the pay roll. It is true that he might meet his classes as discussion groups, but in such a democratic function his prestige and authority would be largely gone, and he could scarcely be happy. It seems altogether likely that he would soon be driven to compose another set of lectures and return to the role in which he first found happiness and fulfillment.

The lecture system is a particularly great advantage to young instructors who have just completed their graduate study and have well-ordered sets of notes from their graduate courses which they can retail to the students. These young men are able in this way to give courses quite as well as the renowned scholars under whom they have taken their work. Through the miracle of the lecture system, the great thoughts of master minds are thus broadcast in the academic world in ever-broadening

circles. Only a radio hookup could do the work so ef-
fectively.

But the lecture system is a blessing likewise to the
students. Some educators insist that the students should
themselves read the books rather than listen to the professor expound their contents; but such men do not realize how busy the students are and how exhausted they
often are after attending to fraternity activities, pep
meetings, class politics and vacations. As a great educa-
tor once said, the greatest need of American college students is sleep, which they can often get in class better
than anywhere else. If by reason of professorial exaction
or insomnia the students cannot sleep in class, they can
at any rate rest while listening to the somnolent hum of
the professor's voice. Many students even learn to take
notes while in a state of complete relaxation, or even in
a coma; or they may avail themselves of the economics of
the division of labor and take turns in writing notes on
the lectures. Professors do not encourage this as much
as they should. A classroom in which a professor is lecturing is a very restful place while a building in which
a score of professors are lecturing suggests a symphony
hall with the orchestra playing the *Moldau River.*

There is much economy in the scheme as it now
operates. The professor enjoys reading books, picking
out odds and ends of information, winnowing out facts
and figures and ideas from scattered sources and putting
them together in new and original patterns. He enjoys
this sort of activity and in time becomes very skillful at
it, and in retailing his information to the students; he can
indicate the important points, saving the students the
time and trouble of accumulating unimportant information. If the students were required to read the books

[ 162 ]

themselves, they would have to spend a great deal of time which they need for outside activities; and they could scarcely be expected to enjoy it. Perhaps even worse, they might develop a habit of reading, which would levy so heavily on their time in later years as to compromise their chances of success in life. Not a few students have been ruined in our colleges and universities by learning to read books. One of the great virtues of the lecture system is that it enables students to acquire an education who have never learned to read. Out in the busy world of later life, the radio and lectures at the Rotary Club enable them to continue their educational advancement in a certain fashion, without using the unsociable expedient of reading books.

But if the students were required to do their own reading, they would suffer in still other ways. Many students have defective eyesight which is always likely to grow worse toward the end of the term; and it seems only reasonable courtesy for the professor to do their reading for them. The students would, furthermore, be obliged to do their reading mainly in the library, where the spirit and atmosphere are decidedly gloomy, repressive and unsociable—likely to dampen the spirits of sanguine youth and so to unfit them for the hopeful work-world of later years. For students in a school of business, this would be particularly unfortunate. It is difficult to imagine worse training for the world of business—for buying, selling, promoting, attending conventions—than four years spent largely in the gray silence of a library reading books and magazines.

Many professors make their lectures not only quieting and restful but even entertaining for they have stories appropriately placed among their notes, one to illustrate each point. In their courses there is always something to look forward to every day. In some fraternity houses there are charts of these courses for freshmen, indicating the date on which each story is due. On the dates when particularly good stories are scheduled, many visitors often come to the class to enjoy the lectures. There are some professors who thinks this an undignified use of the professor's lecture period; but education must be sold to the people, and there is no better way than this, perhaps. Not quite all professors have the faculty of making lectures interesting and intriguing, to be sure; but those who have not this ability also contribute greatly to the moral development of the students—for listening to dull lectures, like hard work of all kinds, strengthens the moral qualities of the students, the qualities of tenacity, perseverance and rugged endurance.

Stimulating, scintillating lectures are an indispensable supplement to the textbooks commonly used. It is a standing cause for wonder that professors who can lecture so entertainingly should write dull textbooks; but certain it is that most textbooks are as uninteresting as *Pilgrim's Progress;* and doubtless, if the professors should write their lectures down and have them printed, they would merely produce more textbooks. A worse situation could scarcely be imagined. The glowing personality of the professor would be lacking, the warm intimate individuality that lightens up the discussion even of the most abstruse and complicated problems would be gone. Looking at the situation broadly, we might well say that what the country needs, next to lower taxes, is more lecturing professors and an AAA for output of textbooks.

## The Lecture System

The use of lectures and textbooks has the final supreme merit that it gives the students a fine sense of completion, of having finished, of being done, of having rounded out their intellectual figures at all concave salients. Unlike disorganized class discussions, lectures and textbooks give a complete picture and do not leave the students with a disturbing feeling that their education is still incomplete, that there are still loose ends dangling, that there is still much to learn. Theirs is not an *Unfinished Symphony*. Four years they have spent distending their minds with systematized and organized information, facts and figures; four years they have devoted to the achievement of mastery of their various fields; and when they have sold their textbooks and dropped the last batch of notes into the waste basket, they face the world with the serene confidence appropriate to those who have completed their preparation for a life of service.

One serious difficulty there is, indeed, with both lectures and textbooks: they are soon out of date. Perhaps on nothing is the rate of obsolescence so high as on economic truth, and the rate appears to be accelerating. The professor, of course, keeps abreast of the times in his lectures; and the textbooks are revised every other year, so the students receive only the freshest of material; but a few years after they have been graduated, the knowledge that they accumulated is largely out of date. Some things do not change, it is true. Plato and Aristotle are translated in much the same way from year to year; Adam Smith and Malthus are in the static state; Marshall being now dead, there are no revisions of his work; but the principles of bank management change from year to year; the national debt is revised every month; and the list of alphabetical government agencies changes every week. Much of the up-to-date information that the students gain from lectures and textbooks is stale soon after graduation, or perhaps even before graduation; and the students are faced with the hard necessity of re-education. Just how this can be accomplished is a serious problem. Our graduates, bulging out like bologna sausages with assorted facts and figures, seem generally to lack a capacity for continued development. Perhaps it would be well if the alumni could return to old *alma mater* every few years and take most of their college courses over again, revive and refresh their waning intellectual interests and bring their information down to date; but it is doubtful whether they would find this convenient, or even altogether satisfying. College years are always regarded—in retrospect—as the happiest years of life; but perhaps not many would enjoy reliving them a half dozen times for the sake of keeping abreast of the times. Like sausages, education is subject to the principle of diminishing utility; and the twentieth year in college would not satisfy a very insistent want. Furthermore, the general application of such a scheme would call for a very great expansion of educational plants including professors and fraternity houses. Altogether it seems definitely impractical.

It has been suggested that the graduation fee be raised to include all later revisions of the textbooks so that the graduates might keep their information up to date by home study; but since there would be no professors in their homes to explain and interpret and indicate the important points, this would probably be inadequate. Students who have become addicted to the lectures of professors often seem rather helpless without them.

A method of re-education which has gained prestige in recent years is that known as adult education—carried on largely, of course, by professors. This has not been entirely successful, however, for various reasons. In the first place, adult education courses lead to no degrees; and students are curiously prone to associating education with degrees. Education alone appears to have relatively small interest for them. In the second place, adult education is generally unrelated to fraternities and social activities so the better classes of people find little in it to beguile them. The result is that the adult education movement is often regarded as a movement mainly for the lower classes. If adult education could somehow be expanded to include dancing and bridge, perhaps be organized in connection with the Rotary and Kiwanis clubs, the D.A.R. and the Chamber of Commerce, it would have a wider appeal. And, finally, there is a growing doubt whether adults can be educated. There is some evidence that most of the students, even with their young, eager and plastic minds and despite their attendance on the professors' lectures, largely evade the educational process during their four years in college and that their intellectual disintegration begins the day of the last examination. A few years later they may be past all reclamation.

The lecture system is not the only blessing that we enjoy. As the world slides irresistibly into the abyss of totalitarian barbarism, as free thought and inquiry disappear in one country after another, it is clear that intelligence generally, and particularly economic intelligence, is a quality little to be desired—that the endeavor of our universities should be to turn out graduates who are technically competent but socially as ignorant as possible. Fortunately, we have seen this need and for some years have been adapting our curricula and methods to it.

Walter Lippmann suggests "that the newly educated western men no longer possess in the form and substance of their own minds and spirits, the ideas, the premises, the rationale, the logic, the method, the values or the deposited wisdom which are the genius of the development of western civilization; that the prevailing education is destined to destroy western civilization, and is in fact destroying it." Continuing further, Lippmann insists that "since the vital core of the civilized tradition of the West is by definition excluded from the curriculum of the modern school, the school must sink into being a mere training ground for personal careers. Its object must then be to equip individual careerists and not to form fully civilized men."

We may concede that our education has indeed contributed less than we might wish to the preservation of civilization. We can see the evidence of this in many changes, particularly in the relative decline of colleges of liberal arts and the growth of professional and trade schools. We can see the shifting attitude in economics by comparing the broad social, philosophical, humanitarian viewpoint of Adam Smith, Mill, Marshall or Taussig with the narrow, technical approach of the New School—in the shift from philosophical and historical emphasis to mathematics and physics.

Yet Walter Lippmann doubtless exaggerates the influence of education. Other factors have made their contribution, too; and if our educational leaders have done their part in undermining democratic civilization, they may well be justified by the fact that it is their function to sell education to the people; and it is a fundamental principle of sales promotion that the seller must find something that the people want. The people want money, success and not social intelligence: hence, the shift from history, philosophy and economic theory to home economics, sales promotion, advertising, salesmanship and business correspondence. And we do offer courses in social economics, surreptitiously and with the necessary coating of sugar—more, no doubt, than our students really want if less than we would need if we wished to save what we are accustomed to call western civilization.

On the whole, the outlook for the lecture system is not as bright as we might wish. Already there have been suggestions that the radio or the victrola be used for lectures to all the students of all the universities; and, of course, either of these would gravely curtail the opportunities for lecturing and would rob the educational process of that priceless ingredient—the personality of the professors, although it would presumably raise the quality of the lectures. A more serious threat is that of the talking cinema and television which would carry not only the scientific content of the lectures but the mannerisms, gestures, smiles and frowns and vocal intonations of the professor as a personality and, unlike the radio could be used in explaining graphs and mathematical formulae. The cinema and television are indeed being used to a limited extent for lectures, and their use may spread to the classroom where they might prove more attractive than lectures by corporeal professors since only a few of the most glamorous and magnetic professors would be employed.

[ 169 ]

A still greater threat is that gorgeous and glamorous movie stars might be employed to learn and deliver the lectures. Imagine Marilyn Monroe delivering a lecture on, let us say, "The Indeterminateness of Price in Oligopolistic Competition"! Imagine the most erudite and eloquent professor facing that sort of competition! Here is surely a dark cloud on our horizon. With the cinema or television a very few stars could give all the lectures needed, and the lectures could be given year after year for films would last a long time, perhaps longer than most professors' notes. Let us be on our guard! As the danger is great, so must our vigilance be unremitting; and our war cry may well be: "The lecture system: it must and shall be preserved!"

# THE AMERICAN HOMO SAPIENS: OR IS HE HOMO "SAP"?

*An address delivered at an Honors Day banquet, University of Nebraska.*

I t was some years ago when ex-President Calvin Coolidge made his famous statement, "The country is not in good condition"; but Mr. Coolidge did not live long enough to see a country and world in really bad condition. We have won or at any rate ended, actually if not officially, the Second World War at a cost of a million casualties and several hundred billion dollars. Yet we have armies in various parts of the globe and are planning for the Third World War as soon as we can get the budget a *little more than* balanced and can find a new crop of boys to do the fighting—a defensive war, of course, to be fought only for the preservation of democracy wherever it is to be found and wherever there is not too much of it; to be fought only as a way of preserving the peace, of course, for we are a peace-loving people and will be obliged to knock hell out of any other people who do not like our peace, particularly if that nation should happen to be communistic. We

are not only peaceful; but we are willing to work unselfishly to achieve our peaceful goals, if we can find out
what the goals are.

Domestically, the skies are moderately serene or
would be if we could find three or four million more
jobs, reduce taxes, balance the budget by giving away
a few billion dollars worth of federal assets, pay a few
dollars on the debt, eliminate a few hundred bureaus
and a few million bureaucrats and provide more government pie for everybody, build up better military protection for less money, give the returned soldiers each a
bonus, an education and a government loan, give the
farmers a subsidy, paid from Heaven, to preserve their
individualism when farm prices fall, build ten million
new homes for ten million vagrants at prices not more
than twice what they can pay, expand social security
provisions to cover the people who are not related to
senators or congressmen, guarantee genuine collective
bargaining by abolishing the closed shop, labor unions,
strikes, picketing and labor dictatorships, raise the tariff
and restore international trade, keep the price level
from rising or falling or wobbling too much, and insure
two new cars in every garage and two chickens on every
car and in every pot.

We not only would like all these things, but we
really have promised them. America is the promised
land; our people are the promising people; ours is a
promising era: that is, somebody is promising most
everybody something or everything. Now, our great
general problem is that of living up to all the promises
that have been made.

All this raises the great overshadowing question of
human rationality, the question whether our people can

ever develop the civic intelligence needed to operate our vastly complicated, integrated economy. To some not unworthy souls the question will, of course, seem fatuous or frivolous. Of course we can, for have we not been operating successfully for 160 years, even in Democratic administrations? I will begin by insisting that the history of the past 160 years proves nothing. During those halcyon years the government did very little very badly, and we did not need much public intelligence. We were operating under the good old doctrine of Adam Smith that every man in nursing his own self-interest was guided by an invisible hand to serve the public interest as well and by the Jeffersonian doctrine that the least government was the best government. Following such simple principles we really did not need any public intelligence at all, and we did not have much. On the few government functions that were undertaken, the people voted wrong as often as right —which I will not press to the further logical conclusion that a nation of idiots would have done as well since idiots would presumably have voted right half of the time. I will not go so far because I could not then explain why political institutions are on a higher plane today.

Although this was unfortunate, it was not fatal as long as there were no critical problems that had to be solved. We could get along. Today we have questions that will not down, that must be solved. Domestically, we must soon solve the question as to where we want to go and how we are to get there. If I sense the tempers of many people, particularly in the Middle West, I believe they think they want to go back, back to the good old days of rugged individualism. That seems a noble ambition, but to achieve it we should have to remake the economic landscape. We would have to smash monopoly, for the General Motors Company does not really represent rugged individualism. We should have to break up all great business combinations, all holding companies, and forbid interlocking directorates, intercorporate stock holdings—all the devices used to stifle individualism. We should have to abolish trade associations, merchant councils, chambers of commerce, farm bureaus, 4-H clubs, the Rural Electrification Administration, the AAA, the Soil Conservation Service—to mention only a few of the cooperative and government organizations that have undermined our individualism. The farmer would have to depend on his own strength and courage in the next slump in farm prices. We should have to smash most of the labor unions, abolish social security, old age pensions and a host of other social services offered for the benefit of labor.

This is the general program—a program for individualism. Who wants to go back? No one, of course! But a lot of lovers of individualism and freedom and private enterprise and the American Way are going to be surprised to find it out. They don't want to go anywhere else either, and they seem determined not to stay where they are. I think they're badly confused and may be lost.

In the international field, public rationality is perhaps even lower and confusion worse confounded. After suffering a million casualties in fighting fascism—at any rate that's what many of us thought we were fighting —we find our government bolstering up fascism and reaction in many parts of the world, indeed almost everywhere that we have any influence. Proclaiming our devotion to the principles of democracy and our undying hostility to dictatorship, we back with money or moral support such unprincipled dictators as Franco, Kai-shek, Rhee and Trujillo. In a death struggle with the unprincipled criminals of the Kremlin, we offend and antagonize friends everywhere and add millions to our enemies.

In planning for the next war we are similarly confused. We don't want another war; presumably, that is, most of the people appear to think that they think they don't; but at the present time they acquiesce in policies which make war likely if not inevitable. We must have peace; and the theory appears to be that the best way to get peace is to act as warlike as possible, send truculent notes to the nations that we don't like and announce our hegemony over a few oceans and over choice real estate scattered from the South Pole to the Aleutians and from Korea to Azerbaijan. Such a policy has been tried a hundred times since the time of Alexander the Great, and it always resulted in war. Perhaps this time it won't. There is nothing aggressive about this, of course. Our army is needed in self-defense just as the great Russian army is. We don't even know just what the function of an army is in atomic war; but perhaps we could hide it in a safe place somewhere. In any event the army officers lend a fine swanky dignity to our social life; and in peace the army might serve well, cooperating with the FBI, in protecting us from the communists and from such new dealers and bureaucrats as may still be hiding in the bushes.

Before the atomic age, such public confusion was not fatal. We could survive wars. Today the scientists

are agreed that a bomb war would be so utterly destructive that it would leave little of what we have called
civilization or even that it might destroy most human
life. The crucial question then is: Can we develop the
knowledge and rationality that we must have in the
atomic age? It is the thesis of this paper that Americans
do not have any such knowledge and rationality today
and are unlikely to develop it. Oscar Asmeringer wasn't
too far wrong when he once said that if there were ten
wrong ways to do anything, and one right way, the
Americans could be trusted to try all the wrong
ways first.

Rationality in the ordinary affairs of life is nothing
to be hilarious about in this land of the brave and free
and fuddled. This is the land, mark you, where the
people pay taxes for the support of medical schools and
services, then permit the radio salesmen to sell carloads
of injurious drugs and patent medicines; where the
radio patent medicine show is the peoples' most valued
entertainment; where farmers sell their good corn and
wheat and buy back, at twice the price they received,
the chicken feed which, although no better than what
they sold, is guaranteed to cure all poultry diseases
from roup to cholera. It is the land where any politician
can ride into office by trumpeting his undying opposi-
tion to grade labeling which, although or because it
would enable consumers to know what they were buying, would destroy American liberty, incentive and
enterprise, the American Way of Life, the Constitution,
the freedom of the press and all the other freedoms
guaranteed by the Constitution, the FBI and the Dies-
Rankin-Thomas-McCarthy-Committee. It is the land
where for several years students were obliged to go

without textbooks in order that there might be plenty
of paper for the advertising of automobiles that were
not for sale and liver pills and fat reducers that *should
not have been* for sale.

On this general point, I found the following not
long ago:

"Though man a thinking being is defined,
Few use the grand prerogative of mind.
How few think justly of the thinking few!
How many never think, who think they do!"
(from *Morals and Manners*, Jane Taylor—1783-1824)

"But the relatively high spending power of the top
bracket of incomes should not deceive the ad man as
to what type of human being he is dealing with. The
very large majority of the American race in every
income bracket are simple, elemental people and 'few
use the grand prerogative of mind.' There seemingly is
no culture and intellectual competence in the United
States that corresponds to our high material standard
of living.

"Nowhere else in the world, outside of this land
of milk and honey, is there to be found a people blessed
with so many automobiles, so many bath tubs, so many
telephones, so many washing machines, so many electric
refrigerators, so many streamlined gadgets for streamlined living. But nowhere else, either, are there to be
found so many millions of *favored* people so spiritually
and intellectually starved, so lacking in a satisfactory
philosophy of living, so devoid of anything that even
approaches a rich inner life. Nowhere else in the world
are there 30 million radio homes, but nowhere else do
15 million housewives listen pop-eyed every day to the
appalling 'soap opera.' Nowhere else . . . do so many

millions of people consider the exploits of Dick Tracy and the uncouth oafs in Moon Mullins to be matters of greater consequence than the Atlantic Charter and the Dumbarton Oaks conference.

"What is America achieving in terms of human values? Are we, as a correlative benefit, witnessing an upsurge in the character of the common man that corresponds to his amazing technological development? Is he in his philosophy and mode of life as 'alert,' 'intelligent,' 'creative,' and 'intent,' . . . as he is behind the drill, the ledger, or the plowshare? Is this war-time common man of ours, so highly eulogized by press, pulpit, pundit, and politician, *off his job* becoming a citizen of equivalent rising stature? Does his dramatically demonstrated genius for mass production, his growing technical skill, his remarkable capacity for 'getting things done' mean that he is (or is surely becoming) a *thinking* human being? Are we, under the whip of war, developing in our factories and in our offices a new race with a new conception of the real meaning of 'civilization'?"[1]

The answer is no, of course; and this was written, if you please, not by a red-eyed communist or a cynical intellectual but by a prosperous advertising executive whose success has presumably been due to accurate appraisal of the mass mind and whose general conclusion, God help us, is that most advertising aims too high, assumes too much rationality on the part of the masses.

The American "homo sapiens"—or shall we say "homo sap"?—is less sophisticated in economics and politics than in his ordinary living as the evidence abundantly proves. Let us remember that the fantastic Townsend Plan and the Ham and Eggs Plan enrolled

---

[1] Woolf, J. D., *Advertising to the Mass Market*, pp. 4, 5.

nearly half of the voters in some communities; that the Ku Klux Klan captured some state and many local governments as a scheme for the preservation of Christian Americanism! Let us remember how in 1933 the people burst into a flame of hope and enthusiasm at the creation of the NIRA which had been borrowed from Mussolini's bag of tricks. In 1932, they voted Hoover out because they had no money with which to buy meat and because the government wouldn't "do anything"; and in 1946 they voted the Democratic Congress out because there wasn't any meat to buy and because the government, the bureaucrats, were doing too much. In 14 years the people had apparently learned that if they are to eat meat there must be both meat and money and that what the government does is not done in a vacuum but through bureaus and bureaucrats, which they don't like. Beyond these, I am not sure just what they have learned.

Some of the polls in recent years do not enhance the picture of the sapient American. According to one poll a few years ago, only 23 per cent of the Americans had a reasonably accurate idea of the content of the first ten amendments of the Constitution, a similar number had never heard of them, and the remaining 54 per cent either could not identify them or gave confused information. Presumably they all knew, however, that these amendments were the basis of American democracy. A poll by the *Denver Post* once disclosed that "while 81 per cent of the persons reached could identify Dagwood Bumstead, a comic-strip character, only 30 per cent could identify the names of the candidates for statewide office." A poll by the *Philadelphia Bulletin* revealed that "four out of five Philadelphia voters do not know the names of Pennsylvania's major party candidates in the current campaign." One pollster claimed that Elsie, the Borden cow, was recognized by 5 per cent more people than could identify Eisenhower and by 10 per cent more than could identify Einstein; but that seems hardly credible.

In *Time*, May 22, 1944, an analysis of polls indicated that 27 million people did not know that the Japs had taken the Philippines, that 54 million had never heard of the Atlantic Charter, that 85 million did not know what a reciprocal trade treaty is, that two thirds of the population did not know that the United States had received reverse lend-lease from Britain, that more than half the adult population did not know that the United States never belonged to the League of Nations. Another poll revealed that while 85 per cent of the people favored the restoration of international trade and amity, most of them were opposed to tariff reduction. In January, 1946, only 31 per cent of all voters knew that elections for Congress were going to be held in November. At the end of the 1944 presidential campaign, only two thirds of the voters could name the Republican vice-presidential candidate and even less could name the Democratic candidate.

People might be pardoned for being unable to name their senators and representatives, for some of the senators and representatives aren't worth naming; but the people chose them and have no right to complain of their own choices. The cook should be willing to eat her own dinner.

We need not use polls to prove the infantile political intelligence of the American. It is a commonplace among social scientists that before the time of Franklin

*The American Homo Sapiens*

Roosevelt there were usually no significant issues in presidential election; they represented mere shadow boxing between two men both controlled by the same powers. Yet, the people were quite satisfied to cast their vote—really believed that they had a vote. They chose between Harding and Cox. They elected Harding, and it soon appeared that he was the worst of the two, but we can't be sure about that. In the next election they were offered the privilege of choosing between Calvin Coolidge and John W. Davis of the distinguished firm of J. P. Morgan and Company—two men very similar in economic views if very different in exterior appearance, both chosen by the same economic powers. Four years later we had a little more choice between Herbert Hoover and Al Smith. Then came Franklin Roosevelt whose great crime appears to have been not that he was a poor economist but that he tried to make the Democratic party follow a somewhat liberal policy, tried to offer the voters a real choice. In this he was not successful; for when the supernumerary suckers of the social substratum evinced strong approval of the communistic New Deal, the knights of rugged individualism and free enterprise, Landon, Willkie and Dewey, were obliged to offer the voters a New Deal too. So the election became a contest in expanding and elaborating the communistic New Deal, and the voters had no real choice again. On Roosevelt's death, both parties turned back; but the Republican party turned back fastest and farthest and with the most joy. Under Truman we had more than one party, but not quite two—perhaps we should say that we had about a party and a half, or perhaps 1.3. I believe most of the people were reasonably happy with this arrangement.

It is really too generous, however, to concede that we ever had two parties at any time. What do we mean by a party? Ordinarily we mean a political organization the members of which are united by common aims, ideals and interests; and if we use this definition we find that we have not had even one party. In what is called the Republican party we have had enrolled such men as Senator Norris who was really a moderate socialist and Senator McCarthy who sounds a little like an echo of Adolph Hitler. Surely that can't be a political party. That's an *assortment*. In the Democratic party, similarly, Roosevelt tried to keep at peace such fascistic reactionaries as Rankin and Bilbo with such liberals as Wagner and Barkley; and that isn't a party either. That's an optical illusion, or a political delusion; or perhaps it's a snare. But the people think it's a party, and some really like it.

Perhaps someone may be so careless of the proprieties as to suggest that the voters have usually had the privilege of voting Socialist if they did not like the Republican-Democratic party; but we can dispose of that argument very easily. Americans do not raise their children to be Socialists.

In state and local elections, even more definitely, there may be only one party; and if there is a pretense of two parties, there is usually no real issue. Yet, most of our people are perfectly satisfied with such disfranchisement. In Kansas, I am told that there is really one machine—a Republican-Democratic machine—in which the Republicans are, of course, disproportionally strong but may support carefully selected Democrats. Whenever there is a threat of a real issue, someone yells "prohibition," and the people organize crusades to seek out the bootleggers, some with the purpose of hanging them, others with the design of buying their products before risks and prices go up. Other issues are forgotten.

In my county, as in Russia and in Germany under Hitler, we usually have only one candidate for some of the offices. While we have a few Democrats in the county who are permitted to sleep in the hotels, eat in restaurants and vote when there are any Democratic candidates to vote for, we would not invite them to our homes nor patronize them in business. In the South this is, of course, reversed.

Since there are no economic or political issues in most elections, our choices must be based on various personal qualities, accomplishments and achievements. In Kansas, choices are often made on the basis of the length of time the candidates have served the Republican party. In Alabama, vice versa. Accomplishments such as music and dramatics are very important. We have had a number of men in Congress and in state legislatures who won their seats through exceptional talent in crooning, in singing cowboy songs or playing boogie woogie. If this suggests infantile political standards, it proves also that Americans have a deep interest in cultural matters.

I sense the question that comes to your minds: "What is wrong with all this?" Surely it is a fair question, and the answer is not simple. Our people appear to be happy and contented with this situation, unperturbed for the present by the troublesome questions which harass more sophisticated peoples. Let us remember that whoso increaseth wisdom increaseth sorrow. Let us remember the matchless distinction lent to German culture by the one-party system of Adolph Hit-

ler, by the great principle of *Gleichanschauung,* of unity
and homogeneity. There are many advantages in homogeneity of economic views. In the first place, it makes
a nation more puissant in glorious war as Germany under Hitler so well proved. In the second place, if all
the people have the same opinions, the same ideals and
aspirations, they can all be made happy by the right
governmental policies; whereas, if the people have different ideals, some will always be unhappy. In Kansas,
all the people want what the Republican party offers
and are happy together except when the Democrats win
an occasional election. In Alabama, the people want
what the Democratic party wants them to want and
are always one happy family together because the
Democratic party always gives them what it wants
them to want, and therefore, what they do want. So
unity and homogeneity are the first requirements for
the happiness of the people.

On the other hand, it must be conceded that this
economic and political unanimity and homogeneity
carry a suggestion of homogeneous imbecility. Complete
homogeneity is more characteristic of termites and sheep
than of men, and not entirely characteristic of sheep—
else there would be no need for sheep dogs to keep the
flocks together. Men who think almost surely come to
various different conclusions. Some men, furthermore,
would rather enjoy the "grand prerogative of mind" and
be sad and troubled than forego the uses of the mind
and be happy—would rather be sad philosophers than
happy fools. There is little place in American society
for such men, and perhaps it is well that there are few
of them.

In some foreign countries there are many men of

this sort. In Sweden, for instance, in the upper chamber there were, in 1945, 84 Social Democrats, only 28 Conservatives, 27 Agrarians, 14 Liberals, and 3 Communists. In the lower chamber there were 115 Social Democrats, 39 Conservatives, 35 Agrarians, 26 Liberals and 15 Communists. These majority Social Democrats lean strongly toward socialism—mind you, they are really worse than New Dealers; and no one has been able to tell why, with so many radicals and communists among the people, Sweden has been able to solve her economic problems better than we have. Perhaps it is their widespread habit of thinking. At any rate, it is fortunate that the Swedes do not live in the United States because most of them would be under investigation by the FBI and by our various congressional Gestapos. Some of them would be in jail. Other Scandinavian countries present the same picture of radicalism and yet appear to solve many of their problems better than we do.

Doubtless most Americans believe that they would rather not solve their problems than have to solve them by thinking, if thinking is likely to lead to radicalism. But I fear that their moral stamina will break down in the first depression. If and when a real depression strikes, there will be some six million farmers, or their representatives, in Washington demanding subsidies on farm products, or perhaps even the slaughter of more poor little pigs. There will be a million or two businessmen in Washington calling for higher tariffs, for government guaranty of profits, and perhaps even for a new OPA or NRA or RFC to keep prices up. And all the people will join the FBI and the congressional Gestapos in a patriotic hunt for the witches and communists who have wrecked our prosperity, while the shades of

Franklin Roosevelt will have their first good laugh since V-Day.

Why are our people that way? Why do they have so little political sophistication; why are they so adverse to the use of their brains in anything but business? They are said to be created in the image of God—I hope that isn't blasphemy—and so they must surely have the capacity for political cerebration. The Scandinavians, who seem to have the same cranial measurements as ours, can think about public questions and appear to enjoy it. Why is it impossible for Americans to do this?

Clearly we cannot blame our teachers. Outside the better universities, many of them—I mean the teachers in the social sciences—are indeed not much given to lucubration or cerebration and are largely innocent of ideas. We cannot criticize them, for that is the reason they were hired, and that is the reason they are not fired. Our public schools and most colleges are not established to educate the youth but to inoculate them against the habit of thinking about important questions; and the teachers properly do what they are hired to do. They are merely retailers of the ideas that are handed to them by influential business groups, propagandists for the status quo and protectors of American rugged individualism, guarding against witchcraft, communism, socialism, anarchism, radicalism, New Dealism and all forms of sin and subversion. Ideas are dangerous to the masses of the people, particularly to the youth whose eager, plastic minds make them highly susceptible to evil influences. If our teachers permitted students to develop a habit of thinking, how could they be sure that the students would come to the right conclusions— the right conclusions being, of course, those held by the

wiser and wealthier and more successful members of
our society? No, the teachers must prevent students
from thinking about important questions.

In spite of our best efforts, we fall short of complete
success in our work for there is evidence that despite
all our precautions, education tends to develop radicalism in our students. Professor Goodwin Watson's
study indicates that radicalism increases with years in
school, from the grades right up to the Ph.D. This appears to suggest that if we wish to eradicate radicalism
our best plan would be to close all schools, or at least
eliminate the study of the social sciences. The latter
course would not solve the problem entirely, however,
because there are radicals in English departments, in
psychology, philosophy and in foreign languages. Perhaps we should have to eliminate the study of literature,
or at least choose with care the books that students are
permitted to read—avoid such subversive literature as
Aristophanes, Juvenal, Voltaire, Heine, Mark Twain and
Steinbeck. In some schools this is being done with considerable success.

Professor Watson announces a further conclusion
from his statistical study—that there is apparently a
correlation between mental alertness and radicalism.
His final conclusion is that we could eliminate about
90 per cent of the radicals from our universities if we
would shut out all who *can* pass the rapid reading test.
Even if we concede the truth of this, we need not con-
clude that teachers should have the credit or the blame
for such radicalism, such political heterogeneity as we
have in the schools. The teachers can hardly shut out
of the schools all students who enjoy thinking, nor can

they be held responsible for the conclusions that they come to.

No, our intellectual unity, homogeneity and aridity cannot be credited to the teachers. Little of our education is done by teachers. Most of it is done by the radio, by the newspapers, particularly by the comic strips, by the popular books and magazines and by the movies. These potent educational agencies reach all citizens with their promotional work for health, cheer, soap, individualism, tooth paste, free enterprise, chicken feed and Americanism. Consider Li'l Abner, the inspiring story of homespun American individualism, seen and read by 27 millions every week; Dick Tracy, ditto; on somewhat the same level Westbrook Pegler and George Sokolsky. Here are unifying educational forces of real significance. So too are our best selling books. Americans like to read the books that everyone else is reading, not mainly because they are interested in them but so that they may engage in cultured conversation at bridge parties. Therefore, if a book becomes a best seller, everyone must buy it; and it becomes an even better best seller. That's why we are individualists. One hundred million Americans, more or less, buy *How to Win Friends and Influence People*, and American manners change over the week-end; a few million copies of *Gone With the Wind* are sold, and the story of the Civil War has to be rewritten; the *Saturday Evening Post* publishes the story of a Trotskyite refugee from Russia, and the Congress meets in special session to consider war with Russia; the movies present *The Bells of St. Mary's*, and the Catholic Church adds a night shift to handle the increased business; or a movie presents Clark Gable sleeping in his shorts and 30 million pajamas and night gowns are torn into scrub rags. Perhaps I exaggerate a trifle, but here are the educational institutions that make the people of our fair land intellectually homogeneous and homochromatic.

The worst difficulty with our unthinking political homogeneity is that it won't solve difficult problems either domestic or international. It has never been wise to trust children with firearms, and it can be only the most disastrous folly to trust any uninformed and unthinking electorate with such a weapon as the atomic bomb. But any intelligent policy of dealing with this immeasurably destructive weapon must rest on a broad public understanding of foreign affairs which is certainly not in evidence today. Ignorant and unscrupulous politicians in Congress, confident of the backing of their constituents, have been kicking the subject about in legislative halls and committee rooms with careless abandon, as if it were of no more importance than the appropriation for building a lake for a senator.

It is not a cheering picture of American democracy; but perhaps, after it has grown worse for a few more years, it will improve when our students get out into action. There is, of course, little we teachers can do. I can only suggest a choice among three possible courses, all bad. You can, in the first place, stand on the sidelines and watch the procession go by and get whatever fun you can out of the antics of the crowd. Or, you can try to get the people to take an interest in public affairs, perhaps even try to teach them some of the elementary facts and principles. If you do this you will probably be crucified, but you may have the satisfaction of knowing that perhaps long after you are dead and buried in infamy you will come to be regarded as a great hero or saint and that books may be written about your noble career and your heroic sacrifice. It is a career which, in anticipation, makes the spine tingle and the heart beat faster if you have a suitable spine and heart. Safer it would be, I shall not say better, to follow a third course—join the cheery, carefree throngs that are hurrying to their atomic graves, singing a pot-pourri of the *Star Spangled Banner, Horst Wessel,* and *The More We Get Together the Happier We'll Be.* Unless the American can somehow develop a much higher level of political perspicacity, it doesn't make a lot of difference what anyone does, providing he has high standing with Saint Peter.

. . . the university with the biggest bull would be the greatest university; and, of course, the bull would be free of difficulty with grades.

# THE SALES PROBLEM IN AMERICAN EDUCATION

*An address delivered at the dinner meeting of the Midwest Economics Association, 1950.*

In a summer in Denmark, I found the Danish attitude toward education one of the most interesting aspects of the life of that most civilized and enlightened country. At a party at Haslev one night, I met some of the high school teachers. About half of them were men, and they were not timid and furtive but upstanding, confident, reasonably well-dressed, scarcely distinguishable outwardly from the American Rotary elite. I asked one of them how men could be induced to go into teaching. He looked puzzled but explained that teaching, even in a high school, was a good life, even honorable. I asked him if teachers did not hold a precarious tenure, were not likely to be fired for entertaining and expressing wrong opinions on important questions. Again he seemed puzzled, looked at me as if I might have crawled out from under a rock; but said, of course, no teacher was ever dismissed for anything but incompetency. In short, teaching in Denmark is a respected vocation, teachers are respected, and education is a respectable business.

But to avoid possible misunderstanding, I must define my terms. By "education" I do not mean training in the vocational and trade schools that enroll most of the students in what Americans call universities—in engineering, law, pharmacy, business, agriculture, medicine and dentistry. For the present, let us call that "training" even though we do slip some educational work into the curricula of these schools. Our engineers often take as much as three hours of economics. Neither can I include here all the work in literature and the humanistic studies except as far as it tends to develop a broad and generous social philosophy. Education of this sort is partly or largely a consumers good, designed to build richer if not happier lives; and it is surprisingly well done—in spite of the fact that the American social milieu is rather hostile to such work. The people are not opposed to it but regard it as of only decorative significance. By education, in the present analysis, I mean *training students to think judiciously and sanely about important social, economic and political problems—making intelligent citizens of them.* It is education in this sense that the Americans desperately need but do not usually tolerate; it is education in this sense that the Scandinavians carry on supremely well.

Americans have always been deeply interested in schools. They tax themselves heavily to build fine school buildings, especially the gymnasiums around which American intellectual life largely focuses, buildings which have somewhat the same significance in the physical, intellectual and spiritual landscape as the cathedrals of France and Italy. A Scandinavian visiting America and seeing our splendid school buildings would as-

sume that we had almost a *reverence* for education; but
he would be as badly mistaken as most Americans are;
he would not see what a hollow shell, what a spurious,
hypocritical façade much of the business is. Americans
spend much hard-earned money for schools, but most
of them are opposed to education in the sense in which I
have defined it.

In the public schools they pay teachers somewhat
less than plumbers earn for the reason, of course, that
education is regarded as less important than plumbing;
they require teachers to live in social goldfish bowls so
that their morals may be constantly supervised. Teachers must maintain high moral standards. (How they can
do it with students around is a mystery.) The people insist that teachers must hold satisfactory views on all important questions—in religion and politics, for instance,
for the freedoms guaranteed by the Constitution are not
accorded the teachers. The teachers must be much hard-
ier than university teachers for they must teach five or
six hours a day, grade papers at night, teach Sunday
school classes on Sunday and supervise student morals
at all times. They must be docile and obedient and cooperative in their relation to the superintendent and
principal, must not assume that they have all the rights
and privileges of organized truck drivers or plumbers or
hod carriers. They are only teachers, and Americans do
not regard teachers very highly.

We of the economic priesthood have the most difficult task in the business world because we are trying
to sell consumers something that very few want. Producers of bread, automobiles, radios, tobacco and whisky have an easy job. Consumers want their goods. Sur-

geons have no difficulty selling their operations to consumers who want to be restored to health; lawyers may
be viewed with suspicion but men who are in trouble
really need and want their services; life insurance salesmen provide desired security against the various hazards
of life; preachers easily sell security against later hazards
to men and women for whom life insurance and social
security do not run for a long enough time. In some cases
the producers are obliged to create the want to be satisfied; but the advertisers are skilled at this business; and
having created the want, the sales problem is not difficult.

We must concede that our product is not such as to
attract indifferent purchasers. We try to sell education
as elaborated in textbooks which are commonly the most
perfunctory type of literature offered for sale—the type
that no one would conceivably read without compulsion.

Even our textbooks are, however, models of clarity
and interest compared with some of the late models of
theoretical analysis. The fearful jargon of much of the
"new economics," like the incantations of Zulu witch
doctors, is calculated to frighten many prospective purchasers away from our most interesting and once popular study. Such a jargon is indeed appearing in most university studies and is probably inevitable, even necessary, as scholars enlarge their knowledge and refine their
analysis. Much of the recent theoretical work in sociology and psychology, as in economics, is unintelligible to
any but a few professors in the field, if to anyone. Indeed we may look forward confidently to a time when
laymen will be able to understand little or nothing that
professors say or write, and for economics that will be
at least unfortunate since much of our economics can be

of use only if realized in legislation—which means that it must be intelligible to legislators and to their constituents. Of course, if we can make an exact science of economics, as some of our younger messiahs now promise, so that it will be of reliable use to businessmen and politicians and particularly to speculators in the stock and exchange markets, we would not want it to be understandable to the vulgar masses. We will then be a new priesthood with a recognized monopoly of the way of salvation. But when I consult three or four priests of the New Exact Science and Faith on a particular question and get three or four different and contradictory views, I gain the impression that the priests are not quite clear as to the way to Heaven and that the sinner seeking salvation will do well to select his priest and his incantation with the greatest care, or that there are many ways of salvation and that it makes little difference which we take. And this is a poor sales argument for any particular brand of salvation or, indeed, for any salvation at all.

In my academic life of some 38 years, I have seen four waves of prophets emerge from the desert crying the wrath to come, proclaiming death or banishment to the senescent and senile disciples of older orders and promising a new faith that would really do miracles. Some 35 years ago, some of the statisticians discovered that economic theory was the futile, fatuous exercise of feeble old men and promised a new scientific economics based on facts. They did indeed find facts and, after some years, learned what to do with some of them. A few years later the institutionalists came forward with the suggestion that all the doctrines proclaimed by the earlier prophets were so much twaddle which must be thrown away before the temple of the true faith could be built. Some years later, Chamberlin and Robinson proceeded to batter at the Paleolithic temple, and some of their disciples declared that it must be totally demolished to clear the way for a respectable edifice. At about the same time another order of prophets announced that the doctrines of the older prophets were of no validity and that only mathematics could cure their vices. And then came Lord Keynes, the Earth-Shaker, followed by an army of adolescents like the Pied Piper of Hamelin, declaring that all earlier faiths were so much sounding brass and tinkling cymbals.

Far be it from me to criticize those who criticize. We are beholden to all of them, but they have undermined the confidence of consumers in our products and have made our sales problem more difficult. Prospective purchasers who are suspicious of our goods anyhow can quote our own dissident disciples to the effect that we are all charlatans dealing in spurious products.

Then, of course, we lecture to students under the lecture and regurgitation system. It is unfortunate that our propensity to lecture is out of proportion to the students' propensity to listen, but the discrepancy is largely made good by the students' propensity to sleep. In Keynesian terms, A equals the professor's propensity to lecture, X the students' propensity to listen, Y the students' propensity to sleep in class, and Z the students' propensity to cut class and sleep in bed. Our equation then is $A = X + Y + Z$.

When the priests disagree, they are always likely to lose custom; and through the present schism in our own study we are, no doubt, losing the confidence of customers and a considerable volume of sales. If there were only two brands of faith, if the Keynesian Kids and the older order of Paleolithic Prophets merely offered two competitive brands of faith without resorting to unethical criticisms of each other's products, buyers might assume that both products were good, might rejoice in the choice offered them—the choice between going to hell by way of Keynesian inflation or by way of neoclassical Paleolithic deflation and stagnation. But the amenities of ethical competition have not always been observed; each of our competing orders has at times hinted that the other is dealing in shoddy doctrine; the Keynesian Kids have rather openly proclaimed that all the prophets from Adam Smith to Marshall, and even down to the year of the Holy General Theory, were fools, numskulls, ignoramuses, nitwits and nincompoops who spent their arid lives looking for the wrong things in the wrong place in the wrong way, finding nothing, but gaining a spurious and transitory glory because there was as yet no prophet of the true faith to show the way of light and life and salvation; and the Order of Paleolithic Prophets have on occasion proclaimed that the Keynesian Youth were false as the Prophets of Baal.

The main difficulty is, however, not in ourselves but in our stars. We are trying to sell something that only a few want, trying to feed the bread of life to students who hunger rather for the fleshpots of bourgeois philistines— or perhaps are not hungry for anything. We have an impossible task. In their homes, these young men and women have absorbed the philosophy of self-help and cupidity, or at least cupidity, the economic doctrines of Hamilton and Hoover or perhaps of Franklin Roosevelt, the moral imperatives of the sanctity of the profit motive and the American Way of Life. In the public schools where the children have been herded by women who combine the functions of nursemaid, missionary, police-matron and perhaps to a limited extent, teacher, the children have largely evaded the educational process although they have been trained in graphic arts, cooking, folk dancing, citizenship, football, basketball and assorted athletics and, having plenty of leisure, have learned to smoke, drink, make love, push the accelerator, talk silly nonsense and otherwise deport themselves as befits leisure classes everywhere. President Colwell of the University of Chicago is reported to have said that our high school graduates are illiterate, quite unable to read and write; but such a statement is exaggerated and likely to be misunderstood. Most of the graduates are indeed illiterate; but, like most young people, they can read books and magazines which are simple and salacious. These young men and women are, however, ill-fitted to follow any educational program; and most of them are not interested in doing that.

The union of football and education is morganatic to the point of miscegenation, a tie so close that it makes Catholic marriage look like rampant free love. College athletics (indeed, are there any other athletics of importance?) are, let us say, the natural and spontaneous manifestation of the instinct for play common in the young of most mammals. A healthy mind in a healthy body, that is the end sought; and the black eyes, broken noses, sprained ankles and charley horses are only the honorable scars won in pursuit of this end, somewhat as in earlier years the clipped ears and noses and scarred cheeks of German students attested their earnest pursuit of knowledge. Athletics is training in citizenship. Of course, our college athletics call for money—it has been rumored that one football team in our valley costs

$200,000 a year—but this is money willingly given by patriotic alumni and well spent for the only thing educational that our alumni are interested in. Here we see the only known important function of alumni, the function which makes it doubtful if it would be wise to poison our students on the day of graduation to prevent them from becoming alumni.

It is sometimes said that there is too much specialization in this athletic business, that only a few develop the splendid bodies in which the minds are developing or are assumed to develop later, while the millions of cheering spectators exercise and overdevelop their lungs. But, of course, specialization is the trend of the times and it cannot be evaded. Furthermore, following the leader in shouting for the team is quite in the American tradition, is excellent training for American citizenship and American cooperative free individual enterprise and for boosting the home town or the home state or valuable real estate anywhere.

Perhaps some other form of citizenship training might be better. Bullfighting would have some advantage in that it would call for fewer performers and so would cost less. Bulls could be bought for as little as $1,000. If half the spectators could be induced to cheer for the bull, the fine emulative spirit of college football could be preserved; the university with the biggest bull would be the greatest university; and, of course, the bull would be free of difficulty with grades. It is possible that this would not interest students as much as some of our athletic battles, but it would be preferred to studying.

Football is a democratic diversion, a substitute for

education which is available to all students irrespective of ancestry, wealth or social grace. Fraternities appeal to a more limited clientele, but for the upper-class students they afford a reason for going to college and an escape from the stifling atmosphere of formal education while they afford moral training of a high order and preparation for life.

No wonder, indeed, that our students prefer the fraternity houses to the classrooms. The houses are more distinguished, more swanky; they speak more clearly of pecuniary reputability and yet they are more restful to the mind; and, as a further advantage, the houses are largely paid for by the parents; whereas, students must do their own studying, if any.

In recent years there has been a remarkable proliferation of professional fraternities, chartered presumably to promote comradeship, competency, high ethical ideals, leadership, citizenship, public spirit, banqueting, dancing and other spiritual ideals and diversions and distractions and, possibly but not certainly, education. The use of Greek letters attests the high character of these organizations; and most students are anxious to join, some because they have achieved no other fraternities, others from the mere habitual and characteristically American propensity to join—as Keynes would express it. They hold meetings where they listen to domestic professors who have been lecturing to them for weeks or to imported professors of distinction or to businessmen of sagacity and substance; and all of them hold national conventions where they consider the problem of maintaining the high standards of the fraternity, whatever that may mean and in whatever respects those standards may be wabbling. Most of the contributions of the members of these fraternities are paid to the national head-quarters to maintain the traveling secretary, inspector, revivalist and missionary and to publish the quarterly herd book which records the distinguished achievements of all the brothers everywhere, with pictures of con-claves and banquets and other festive and intellectual diversions. National organization gives the members a fine sense of dignity and responsibility, of lateral and ter-ritorial expansiveness. The greatest virtue of these fra-ternities, however, is that they offer an occasional release and diversion from the drudgery of formal education and an opportunity for the brothers to get together in a dif-ferent pattern from that of the classroom; and, of course, they face no examinations on the proceedings.

But the students prefer many other things to educa-tion. Much time is given to school politics; and since there are no issues in school politics, this is excellent training for American political life later. The students spend much time in student government where they learn how to run a university, in the Y.M.C.A. and devo-tional and inspirational exercises where devout profes-sors address them on the duties and responsibilities of Christian living. They devote much time to the selection and training of cheer leaders, to the selection of queens for all the festive occasions—there should really be kings too if the royal blood is not to run dry—to house decora-tions for the homecoming, to reunions with the alumni of 20 years earlier whom fraternity members, of course, remember affectionately, and to bull fests on the ob-viously important topics of sex and football. Most stu-dents appear to have a morbid fear of going to bed and do so only after many hours of convivial chatter, and fi-nally of study. A fairly typical day would be: up at 7:45;

breakfast at 7:50; class at 8:00, 80 per cent awake; class
at 9:00, 70 per cent awake; class at 10:00, 60 per cent
awake; class at 11:00, 60 per cent asleep; lunch, 100 per
cent awake; afternoon, study, relaxation and bull fest in
varying proportions according to imminence of next examination; dinner and bull fest, 6:00 to 10:00; and study
until sleep knits up the ragged sleeve of care.

So most of our students do not hunger and thirst for
the intangible riches of intellectual adventure for its own
sake. A few, God bless them, do so and spread a modi-
cum of roses along our barren path; but most of our students are not concerned with the things of the spirit but
seek merely the shortest, speediest and easiest route to
pecuniary affluence—the natural fruit of the crude, soulless, materialistic, machine-ridden, clattering, roaring,
hurrying, price-worshipping philosophy that has provided our fair land with the most cars and the best plumbing and the most radios and the worst broadcasts in the
world, and more and bigger slums and drearier towns
and uglier cities, and more fools driving faster to get to
or away from them, and more red-baiting fanatics and
Gestapos trying to preserve a largely non-existent rugged individualism through tactics borrowed from Hitler
and Joe Stalin. Most of our students are after success and
money; and in response to this demand, we are turning
our universities into agglomerations of trade schools
where we may require as much education as the students
and the people will stand for.

But I cannot well condemn these young men and
women for avoiding education. Studying and thinking
are hard work, not the favorite indoor sports even of
most professors, who are paid for engaging in them. An
educated man or woman would be something of an oddi-

## The Sales Problem in American Education

ty in American society, unlikely to make friends and influence people. In their own interest, young men should avoid education as far as possible; and young women should avoid it in the interest of domestic harmony since they are likely to marry the men. So I do not condemn the students who prefer wealth and ignorance and happiness to poverty and education and distress. After all, wealth may be used for noble purposes, for instance, to add bathrooms in the house. There is a fine spirit of emulation in striving to be a four-bathroom man—or to contribute to the fund for buying football players.

So a considerable majority of our students do not want an education. Unfortunately, almost always in the public schools and rather commonly in the colleges, the school heads themselves are opposed to education, because it causes so much trouble, may even result in job-severance and black-listing. A school superintendent who has been so remiss as to permit educational work in his social science department is likely to lose his job. At best, educational work always interferes with the task of raising money for education because it antagonizes the men and women who as taxpayers or as philanthropists provide much of the money for schools. Rather than engage in such a hazardous activity, many school administrators devote their funds to vocational training which the American public regards with much favor, particularly if it is called education, or to athletics, which has every American virtue, being spectacular and non-educational, or to the maintenance of public relations agencies to raise more money to raise more money to raise more money. Educational work often interferes with this beneficent circle.

Here we see one reason for the multiplicity of bureaus and institutes and departments and offices of all American universities, many of them set up to keep professors away from educational work and to do research for the benefit of some particular influential group or for the general good or harm of all. Often able men are given such work on the general theory that it is very important and demands high talents; whereas, anyone is competent to do the teaching.

Most definitely the outside world, the merchants and bankers and bakers and candlestick makers, do not favor education—in the sense in which I have defined that term; they do not respect either education or educators. There are various reasons for this. In the first place, most teachers are not wealthy, do not have the outward and obvious indicia of pecuniary reputability. Most of them do not even have the physical and personal characteristics that Americans esteem, the pep, fire, vigor, vitality, zest, speed, optimism, bounce, buoyancy and flamboyancy of the better bourgeois classes. On the contrary they are likely to be dyspeptic, anaemic, hollow-chested, hesitant, with a thoughtful droop of the trousers. Americans do not rate such qualities high.

The wives of our professors do not embellish the picture greatly. Some of them are fairly well nourished and not altogether unattractive although they do not have the appearance of social elite; but we must distinguish two general classes. In the first class are those who married for love, who share cheerfully in their husbands' devotion to learning, do not pine for beefsteaks and fur coats. In the second class are those who married professors because they were unable to achieve more successful men, women who saw their arms growing thin, their clavicles protruding, and finally accepted such husbands as they could get. These are not by nature the most beautiful women, and they often wear an expression of stoical resignation or perhaps of furtive and harried indecision as if wondering whether they might not have done better if they had waited a bit longer. Altogether the faculty wives do not enhance the prestige of education with the American public.

What the teachers of social studies teach, furthermore, cannot ordinarily be respected because it does not point the way to profits. Economic or political or social intelligence may be needed to save the nation and the world, but our people are not interested in saving the nation or the world. That, they can turn over to the un-American committees. They are interested in profits and in the objective manifestations of pecuniary success. An intelligent understanding of our foreign policy or of the Taft-Hartley Act has no discernible earning value and, if detected, is likely to arouse public suspicion of communistic subversion. Most intelligent Americans—and this would, of course, include professors of economics— are commonly believed to be communists.

Perhaps we should have to concede that we economists are not very effective salesmen of education for yet other reasons. Teachers are not very great men and women or, of course, they would not be teachers. They are only what is left after the deans have been picked out. Our more ambitious individuals naturally go into vocations that are more respected by the American public—business or the more lucrative professions; those who enter teaching are the ones who can be contented with the pursuit of learning for its own sake or who have not the courage and resolution to do anything more dignified. Furthermore, many teachers are obliged to devote most of their energies to work on committees rather than to selling education. All great universities have many committees of professors which do the unimportant tasks of administration, those tasks which do not seem important enough to engage the attention of the president or deans or assistant-deans or sub-deans or accessory-deans or other administrators or sub-administrators.

Here we see a very serious fault in our methods. We have not the characteristically American booster spirit that powers the spirit of men and gets things done. Perhaps some of you have heard that great Rotary Anthem:

Mighty Union! Glorious Plan!
Worldwide Brotherhood of Man,
Friendship, Service, Liberty,
All are found in Rotary.

Ours the joy to prove the test,
He profits most who serves the best,
Let every brother sing with zest,
Long live the day of Rotary.

Here are powerful crusading faith and consecration, ladies and gentlemen, such as we never bring to our own task! If we could bring the same spirit to play on the promotion of education, we might move mountains or possibly even sell a little education.

Or perhaps we might take a lesson from the fraternities. How often in the stilly night have I heard that moving chorale, sometimes slightly alcoholic:

If you don't be a Beta Theta Pi
Oh, you won't go to Heaven when you die,
When you die!

There is perhaps a measure of exaggeration here,

but surely it is unimportant in relation to the splendor of the general theme.

Similarly moving, inspiring and energizing are those promotional songs of our great industrial firms who seek to serve us by selling us goods the need for which we have seen too dimly or not at all—liver pills, whisky, cigarettes, soap and chicken feed.

> "Feed your chicks Nutrena, Nutrena,
> The best feed that money can buy";

is a characteristic American folk song, as characteristically American as lynching and kidnapping, potent not only to sell Nutrena and to build up the health of our flocks but to energize the farmers who mingle their morning prayers with its haunting melody and then go forth to sow and reap so that there may be food and sustenance for the nations. The American Way! The Best Way! The way of freedom and individualism and enterprise and Americanism and chicken feed! Our people may well lack the political sophistication and sagacity of some of the more enlightened peoples abroad, but surely they have the crusading spirit—or shall we say the propensity to crusade—the ebullient enthusiasm which stirs the hearts of men and keeps the money circulating.

We teachers have no equally effective techniques; we have no song with which to begin our classes or even our festive banquets.

> Education, Education
> Only salvation of the nation
> Men and women of every station
> Without it surely face damnation.

Perhaps this could be improved, but I offer it as a tentative singing commercial for our work, something consistent with American ideals. And I suggest that our loyalty oaths which we take only once are not an adequate substitute for the singing of our national anthems, *America, Home on the Range* and *The More We Get Together the Happier We'll Be.*

A further difficulty is that teachers carry in stock too many differentiated or more-or-less differentiated products. They offer too many courses. Salesmen have long recognized that they must not offer the buyer too many choices lest he become confused and incapable of making any choice at all; but in our universities we offer thousands of courses—and the high schools copy the universities in this—covering every subject that any professor ever became interested in. Whenever a professor learns more than he needs to teach one or two courses he adds another course, not because the students need it but because he thinks he would be interested in teaching it; and so the number of courses increases by geometric ratio as the number of professors increases, to a point where there are not enough students to take all the courses and where, if they take most of them, they do not have time to get an education.

The educational process is such that it could not command the respect of mass-minded Americans anyhow. Education must mean free inquiry, uninhibited study of all aspects of a question; and inevitably it must often lead to many conclusions that the patriotic better classes will not hold dear. An enlightened, liberal-minded people like the Danes can respectfully concede to teachers the privilege of holding and teaching opinions different from their own; but perhaps as a result of the pioneer sport of shouting down the rain barrel, most Americans can tolerate only echoes of their own views; they read only journals which elaborate their own views; they listen only to Charlie McCarthy voices. Particularly is this true of the upper bourgeois classes and of their less successful echoes. They want teachers who will express their own ideas, if any, with force and eloquence; indeed, they insist on it; and, of course, there is some justice in their demand. They pay heavily for the support of the schools, and perhaps they should have the right to say what they get for their money. What would we say of a groceryman who insisted on sending us turnips when we ordered carrots, or of a laborer who insisted on shingling the house when we ordered it painted? If our best people are opposed to education, we should eliminate it; but it would be a purifying experience if we could be honest about it.

If teachers could be induced to serve what the taxpayers call for, they would have a really idyllic life, loved and honored by the better classes everywhere. They would not need to read much—indeed would not dare to read much—for the people do not read much; and reading is likely to lead the teachers away from the generally accepted views. If the teachers did not read much, they would, of course, be less confused and perplexed, much happier and peppier; and they would have more time to develop Christian citizenship in the students, by which, of course, we mean make Republicans of them. The only difficulty would be that many of the students would not listen to them.

But perhaps there are some teachers who do not agree with my thesis that Americans do not respect education and educators, some who really believe that the people regard ours as a noble calling; but we should not be misled by the kindness and courtesy of some of our students who, indeed, may for a few years regard education as a tolerable evil and us vendors as honorable, even if queer. It makes us happy when students come to see us. It builds up our morale and self-esteem. Particularly does it please us when alumni come back and call on us, and after an hour's discussion of the football team, tell us what an inspiration we have been in their lives, how the principles we taught them have lighted up life's rough course and have guided them to higher and nobler ends, how their hearts bleed for the unfortunate masses who never had the privilege of taking our courses. It cheers us to hear such things, and we may even believe them. We may almost get the impression that in providing so much inspiration at so low a cost, we are offering one of the few bargains available in the present inflation. At any rate, the students who treat us respectfully should not mislead us as to the general American attitude.

Americans recognize the advantages of specialization in most kinds of work. If they have car trouble they do not consult the first plumber or painter who happens not to be busy; for an appendicitis operation they do not ordinarily call on a butcher or carpenter; they do not ask a banker to treat toothache, a plasterer to cure cross-eyes, an electrician to treat the dog's distemper. They would think it stupid to do such things. But in the fields of social study, they do something quite like this. They do not recognize any advantage in specialization; anyone knows as much as anyone else or much more if he is superior in one of the only respects in which they recognize superiority—pecuniary success or brass braid.

As practical, patriotic Americans of the better class-

es see matters, economic, political and social problems
are very simple, easily understood. No specialized training is needed to understand them, or indeed, it may
be an obstacle to clear perception and sound judgment.
Generalized sagacity and power such as bankers, grocerymen, lawyers and insurance salesmen develop in
practical business in computing interest, in selling eggs
or insurance, such generalized sagacity as military leaders develop in marching and saluting and planning bat-
tles is a far more powerful tool in analyzing our simple
problems than is the specialized training of the economist and political scientist. So the problem of building
democratic spirit and institutions in post-war Germany
was given to a general of generalized sagacity, steeped
and soaked in the democratic spirit of the army; so the
economic organization of western Europe was a job not
for a specialized economist but for an automobile manufacturer. Western Europe and Studebaker cars are, after
all, very much alike. Both must be organized. So the
economic departments and bureaus in Washington are
mostly headed by advertisers, investment bankers, real-
estate operators and heroes of brass and braid—men of
generalized sagacity rather than specialized and educated men. Some economists and other specialists are
indeed employed, in subordinate positions because, of
course, professors are not skilled in organization.

Even colleges and universities are more and more
seeking as leaders, generals, businessmen, lame-duck
politicians—anything but educated men. One of the
most difficult tasks professors face in such institutions is
that of educating their presidents, a very necessary task
but one that calls for more tact and diplomacy than most
professors can command.

The organization of our schools from the kindergarten to the college proves again that the people do not respect teachers. The public schools are autocracies, officially absolute if, as a matter of practice, not always quite that. The school board hires and fires the superintendent who in turn hires and fires the principals and supervisors and inspectors and snoopers and teachers—subject to whatever restrictions may be set up by communistic teachers' unions—and the autocracy is not always benevolent. The teachers, excepting perhaps the coach, are so many employees, so many lackeys, flunkies, subject to treatment that plumbers or truck drivers would not tolerate. Even the choice of textbooks is subject to the dictation of some sort of board of so-called education composed of men of generalized sagacity. Recently such a state board in one of our states found that the history text used was un-American because it stated that some activities in our sweet land of the free had been socialized. The history teachers thought it was an excellent book, and it might have been assumed that their judgment was good, but the book was dropped. A recent publication of the Chamber of Commerce of the United States carries the title "Socialist America"; but mere teachers and professors should not use such terms. They might not understand all the implications involved.

So are most of our colleges and universities organized as autocracies, in many cases legally absolute like business corporations. This seems logical to most Americans, who are unable to draw fine distinctions, for instance, between education on the one hand and pork or cigarettes or fertilizer or whisky on the other. Production is business, and education is business. At any rate, none of us ordinary professors can have any illusions as to the dignity of our estates. To the administrators we are merely "staff," somewhat like "reserves" to the military or "raw material" to the manufacturer; to some of our students we are a bore and a necessary evil; to many of our patriotic citizens we are damn communist professors. The goods we sell are not generally acceptable, and we are poor salesmen.

I hope I will not be held un-American if I say that all this seems unfortunate. It is fairly clear that Americans are botching some of their most serious problems. For instance, we would like to build up a defense against communism. How would an enlightened people do that? The Scandinavians do it by building up a really fine democracy, so generally satisfactory that the vast majority of people are contented and in no humor to listen to communist messiahs. The Scandinavians appear to believe in democracy and believe that the people are competent to decide matters wisely. Americans have a different line of attack. Fearful of the democracy that they prate about, they abandon as much of it as possible, adopt fascistic expedients and policies as far as the courts and the Constitution permit, in an apparent effort to justify Marxian strictures on capitalism, adopt Stalinist terrorist techniques, espionage and thought control, and conduct themselves generally like the witch-hunters of the time of Cotton Mather. In this way they not only do the Russian dictator the honor of imitation and provide him with excellent propaganda for his newspapers but convey to the rest of the world the impression that we have very little democracy and yet think it is too much. I might cite a score of instances of American boggling of public problems, and the cold war is not all that we are losing.

In such states as Wisconsin there are indeed great patriotic and far-seeing statesmen who are willing to protect their people from the most dangerous forms of innocence and ignorance and lift from their sloping shoulders the heavy responsibilities of democratic citizenship; but in many of our states there are no statesmen competent to do this. At any rate, many people need our product more than they need Lyons tooth paste or Alka Seltzer. Our teeth and livers are in healthier condition than our economy or our politics, but I have no elixir for our economy and politics. Nothing less than a vitalizing, health-giving, vitamin-packed elixir would be acceptable—presumably one which would provide an energizing government handout to every economic class with more than a thousand votes, paid for by God. Nothing less would be acceptable to our stalwart, liberty-loving, individualistic American people; and no economist has yet been able to compound such an elixir. It would be a healthy beginning if our people could be made to realize that they have been hypnotizing themselves with their babble about education, that they really are hostile to any such thing, that their spacious schools are largely an architectural false front, that partly as a result of all this they are among the most innocent economic and political boobs in the world. If we could get only so much across, we might hope to set new sales records notwithstanding our poor salesmanship.

# A PLAN FOR BETTER ATHLETIC TEAMS

*Written for the University of Kansas Jayhawker and copied in the New York Herald-Tribune, December 2, 1952.*

To us who have lived in the sunshine, pride, joy, glory and pandemonium of the glorious football and basketball records of last year, procurement of athletic material looms as our most important academic problem. With men like Griffith and Lovellette we could all be happy, and KU could be recognized as a great university. Yet, to our shame, we have no systematic long-run plan for assuring ourselves of worthy successors of such great men. Phog Allen tells me that he cannot look forward to a repetition of last year's glorious victories—no Lovellettes and no plan for more Lovellettes!

Each year we face this disheartening task of finding great men; each year we are obliged to scour the country for men of great stature and power and asthmatic health who need the bracing Kansas air for recovery; and worst of all, we sometimes fail. We need and must have a long-range program, a program that will assure a steady flow of talent into our athletic teams; and I should like to offer a modest proposal to this end.

My plan, in brief, is that we socialize our great athletes, declare them to be public utilities, put them under the charge of a Public Utility Division of the Athletic Department to be managed like any other public utility that we recognize as essential to our welfare; that the Public Utility Division find suitable mates for them, not sweet, delicate little flowers, not Phi Beta Kappa intellectuals, but women of great strength and stature; and that, to insure a steady flow of power back to KU, the Division should offer suitable bonuses for their children—say $25,000 for the first, $30,000 for the second and up to $80,000 for the twelfth. To make sure that the progeny of such marriages return to KU we should make these payments on the installment plan, conditional on their coming back.

Think what would be our situation if we had adopted such a plan years ago! Take, for instance, one of the giants of years ago, "Big-Six" Lattin—six feet and a half tall, a mighty powerhouse, largely responsible for our victory over Missouri one year. We allowed him to choose his own wife—probably an amiable little thing, I never met her. Result, no more "Big-Six" Lattins! If we had socialized and managed him according to my plan, his children might be coming back now, one each year, to tear our enemies to shreds on the gridiron. We simply can no longer permit individualism in the marriage of our supermen any more than the British allow it for their kings.

Why not go even further? With a steady stream of magnificent young manhood flowing back to KU, we pick out the very choicest men for special consideration, special protection. Of these giants some would be greater than others; and we could make Grade A public utilities of the largest, marry them early to women of very special size and vigor; and so develop a type of supermen, perhaps seven or even eight feet tall. Indeed, why not nine or ten feet tall? Who could set a limit to the possibilities of modern science?

See what the scientists have done with such relatively unimportant products as cattle and hogs and squashes and pumpkins! We could in time develop a new and greater type of manhood, a new elite, a new aristocracy, based on obvious and indisputable physical measurements. In time we could, no doubt, drop all restrictions on marriage, for these new aristocrats would no more marry small women than a British baron would marry an American commoner. Such marriages would in time be regarded as a scandalous sort of miscegenation, a threat to the quality of the race, perhaps more reprehensible than communism.

My plan would have even wider influence. With this new elite visibly and daily before us to see and to worship, we would inevitably develop a new social ideal, the ideal of physical perfection. No longer would our big men and women choose spouses indiscriminately from the little runts and scrubs or from the average mediocrities, however amiable and superficially attractive; they would rather look ahead, and in marrying would consider the kinds of children that they were likely to usher into the world and their effect on the glory of Kansas and the dignity of the human race.

Here emerges a delicate question. Should we content ourselves with one wife for each of these men, and perhaps a dozen children; or should we provide for each perhaps a score of wives and hope for a few score of distinguished children? I have a strong sentimental preference for monogamy for ordinary people, but of course athletic considerations would outweigh other considerations with many people, particularly the alumni. Perhaps monogamy would provide about all the athletes we need.

It will be argued by some that we should try to develop intellectual rather than physical giants. Professors often urge this—self-interest, of course. Some of the students, but doubtless a minority. Not the alumni, certainly. There has been no recorded example of alumni interest in the intellectual life of the University. Not the general public. Who ever saw 45,000 people cheering a professor's brilliant lecture, or a student's brilliant recitation? Do the Chamber of Commerce, the American Legion, and the Rotary Club promote a dinner to honor the Phi Beta Kappa initiates? Does the band play for Coif or Tau Beta Pi initiation dinners?

No, none except a few of the students is interested in that sort of thing. Furthermore, the American of today is very hostile to intellectual activity. It is likely to lead to unconventional views—New Dealism, Socialism, Leftism, Individualism and the like. Why should we try to develop a kind of men and women who would have no proper place in American society?

Perhaps it may be argued that my plan would cost too much; but how could a plan for raising the standard of athletics cost too much? We spend millions, many millions, to improve strains of livestock, fruits, and vegetables; surely a few millions to improve human athletes would not be too much. Our University costs only about six million a year. Why not turn this over to the Public Utility Division of the Athletic Department and make us a really great University? It may sound fantastic, too good to be possible; yet this is the direction in which we are moving! The future holds glorious promise: no more professors, no more boresome lectures, no more textbooks to read, no more slavery to the things of the intellect! Eventually, why not now?

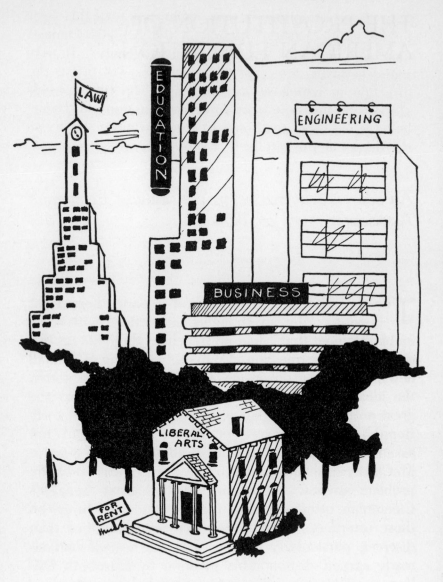

*. . . cluttered up with vocational and trade schools . . .*

# THE PROSTITUTION OF
# AMERICAN EDUCATION

*An address delivered before the Midwest Economics
Association, April 23, 1954.*

The day after I agreed to read a paper here I sat
down to order my thoughts and noticed with some
embarrassment that I had no trenchant thoughts on this
or on any other question. From daily reading of a small
newspaper and a dozen magazines I had indeed gotten
the idea that the suppression of communism was the
great problem in our democratic republic—or shall I say
Republican democracy—but Walter Morton had not
asked for any discussion of that; and of course, Senator
McCarthy has said the definitive word on that pressing
problem anyhow. Rehashing of the great Senator's
Ciceronian utterances was useless; and strictures on
those utterances would have been more valorous than
discreet, particularly for one who like myself had already earned dishonorable mention by Elizabeth Dil-
ling, the *Chicago Tribune*, George Sokolsky and others
of equal standing in the gutter.

Finally it occurred to me that there was a way to

connect the communist crusade with the teaching of economics and business. There, my feet touched ground. There, a great light dawned upon me. The crusade against communism, as carried on in the lunatic asylum formerly known as the United States of America, proves that there should be more teaching of economics while excessive inventories of goods and the threat of a business recession prove that our teaching of business has been unaccountably and unfortunately too fruitful. Here is my theme.

For some years it has been my custom to proclaim the political and economic ignorance of the American people, their inability to understand the complicated economic system that they have built up, the failure of our public schools and universities to take a constructive interest in this problem and the disaster that as a consequence is already upon us. Like Cassandra, I have been preaching this for some years—"preaching" is not far from the right word, and I hope you will forgive me; and like Cassandra I return to the charge.

The evidence of the economic and political illiteracy and confusion of the American people is evident on every hand. Take the Purdue University poll of high school age students which revealed that 58 per cent of the students think the police are justified in giving a man the third degree to make him talk—torture before conviction, a medieval practice. Only 45 per cent believed that newspapers should be permitted to print the news freely except for military secrets; 33 per cent believed that persons who refuse to testify against themselves should be punished severely; 25 per cent would abolish the right of people to assemble peaceably; 26 per cent thought that the police should be allowed to search a person or his home without a warrant. Avaunt with the Constitution! A poll, a few years ago revealed that only 23 per cent of the people polled had a reasonably accurate idea of the content of the first ten amendments of the Constitution; an equal number had never heard of it; and 54 per cent either could not identify it or gave confused information about it. I remember that once in a class of 60 seniors in the University I had some difficulty finding a student who knew as many as two provisions of the Constitution although they all knew, of course, that it was the citadel of our liberties. You have all read, no doubt, of the cynic—probably a communist—who drew up a petition using the words of the Declaration of Independence but could get only two signatures to it because most people thought it was subversive.

Recently the Minute Women of San Antonio have found 600 books in the city library which they proclaimed should be branded as communist—including Einstein's Theory of Relativity—but the mayor insisted that they should be burned. The issue still hangs in doubt; but, of course, book burnings are rather common in our land of the free and fuddled. Perhaps the choicest patriotic item is the proposal over in Indiana that the story of Robin Hood should be expunged from children's books as likely to undermine their reverence for private property. (More recently the Superintendent of Public Instruction has announced that Robin Hood may be read by children if someone sees to it that it is properly interpreted.) A recent statute in California requires the officers of a church, or the members themselves, to take a loyalty oath before the church can be removed from the tax rolls. But some evidences of public insanity are now too numerous to recount, and we must wonder how crazy can a people become. Perhaps we may consider, too, the great truth voiced by Euripides in ancient Athens that whom the Gods would destroy they first make mad.

Such political naïvete goes with an amazing ignorance of history. The *New York Times* cites the results of an American history test given to thousands of college freshmen which revealed that more than 30 per cent did not know that Woodrow Wilson was President during the First World War and that one third did not know who was President during the Civil War.

Today "democratic" America has more gestapos than any other country including Russia; and the manipulators of these gestapos have recently been the dominating figures in American politics; they get more publicity than the President's cabinet, perhaps even than the President, and may well have more power; they frown and reputations wither; they threaten, and all Washington runs for the bomb shelters. Where else but in America (and Russia) could such political gangsters and character assassins become dominating figures? It is true that a victim of this character assassination cannot yet be tortured except mentally; he can only be deprived of his job and denied the possibility of getting another one for which he is trained; guilty or not—and conviction is not strong evidence of guilt— he is only smeared as an actual or potential traitor to his country. Character assassination is the new principle of government in our land of the free and the fuddled—in our land where more money is spent for schools and more pupils go to schools than in any other country.

### The Prostitution of American Education

So our politics is degraded to probably the lowest level in our history—and I have not forgotten the Harding administration with Albert Fall and Harry Daugherty *et al.*—and to a lower level than that of any other enlightened country. We need only to go to Germany before Hitler achieved full power to find something comparable. The resemblances of McCarthy and his crowd to Hitler and his henchmen are closer than most people realize. An English newspaper points out the resemblance of President Eisenhower to Hindenburg and allows Hindenburg the excuse of senility for his failure to save Germany from Hitler. More and more, European peoples find it impossible to understand our crazy conniptions, our ignorance of the principles of decent democracy. It might be argued that the countries of northern Europe, being older, might well be expected to do better; but the truth is that 160 years ago we had probably the most democratic government in the world—today we have the most reactionary government of all enlightened countries. Canada, a younger country than our own, has preserved her democratic institutions; and many Canadians, like some Europeans, view our antics with perplexity and contempt. Writing of the Jenner committee, Colin Cameron, a member of the Canadian Parliament, said: "The first demand of the Jenner committee to be allowed to interview Igor Gouzenko was dismissed here as a piece of gaucherie, stupid and in bad taste but not of very great importance. The second demand, in the face of the refusal of the Canadian government to accede to the request and its expressed conviction that Gouzenko had no further information to offer the committee, was regarded here as a piece of intolerable impudence. Coupled as it was with an attempt to blackmail Canada with the hint that the committee had some discreditable information regarding the Honorable Lester B. Pearson, Minister of External Affairs, this impudence appeared to be that of the gangster underworld.

"It cannot be emphasized too strongly that Canadians, who have viewed with a hitherto somewhat amused contempt the American practice of trial by legislative bodies, are now aroused to the danger of these practices involving their own nationals."

The *Toronto Globe and Mail* summarized this matter: "It [the Canadian government] should say that if Gouzenko wants to take part in the Jenner-McCarthy vaudeville show he is free to do so—on his own responsibility and at his own considerable risk."

I believe that the powerful pressure of our government finally gained access to Gouzenko, but not to the respect of the Canadians. In short, we have become an object of the suspicion and even contempt of the civilized world. Engaged in a desperate struggle with Russian communist barbarism—the outcome of which no one can foresee—we, by our stupid conduct, alienate friends by the millions, provide our enemies with excellent material for their propaganda, and weaken our case before the tribunal of the world. Posing as the leader of democratic nations, we flout the elementary principles of democratic government. Proclaiming as an American virtue a stalwart individualism, we run about, like frightened cattle, shouting our devotion to the Constitution which we are tearing to shreds as fast as the courts will permit.

It is my own modest opinion that while McCarthy is the most unscrupulous, sinister, notorious, and up to

the present time, most influential of the red hunters—
yet because of his very excesses, his boorishness and
utter lack of a sense of decency—he may finally prove
to be less dangerous than political leaders who seem
intent on "stealing McCarthyism from McCarthy," men
who approve of the work he is doing but don't exactly
like his manners. There are many McCarthyites in this
country who wash their necks and, therefore, may
finally do us more harm than slippery Joe.

Our fault is not just stupidity for we have about the
same cranial measurements, the same I.Q., as the more
enlightened peoples. Our fault is ignorance; we know
so little that is true and so much that isn't true. But
why should we, with the most and the biggest newspapers and the most radios and television sets and the
most and biggest schools and universities, why should
we be ignorant? The answer appears to be that most
of us know few sources of information other than the
newspaper and the radio, and these agencies are not
devoted to public enlightenment but rather, perhaps,
even to public obfuscation. Many newspapers—perhaps
most of them—have supported McCarthy and his ilk,
have betrayed to readers none of the incredible details
of his slimy career, have promoted his fascistic ambitions
and those of others of the political underworld. The
radio generally serves the same ignoble purpose. Only
conservative broadcasters and commentators are usually
employed, only those acceptable to business sponsors.
So it is really business that controls, for most newspapers
are business; and most business is, of course, conservative, some of it pleased with the philosophy of
McCarthyism.

Our schools and universities have largely evaded

their responsibilities in this matter. The public schools
have, of course, never dared to do much but inoculate
their pupils against thinking about important questions.
For 50 years our universities have steadily retreated
from the field of education while adding vocational and
trade schools until today they should scarcely be called
educational institutions. We are concerned less and less
with knowledge and wisdom and more and more with
learning to *do* this, that and the other thing. Teachers
in the public schools do not learn mathematics, French
or biology but how to *teach* mathematics, French or
biology; law students do not study jurisprudence but
how to make money practicing law; most journalists do
not try to learn something to write but how to write
about things that they don't know; our business students
do not seek to get an understanding of the economy or
of business as a whole but how to run a store or keep
books or sell insurance or oil stocks. How to *do*, that's
the educational problem of our practical age. We may
not understand the critical problems of the day, we may
be going to hell collectively, but we're going to learn to
be efficient boobs and make a lot of money on the
way there.

Whether in our business schools we do a better job
in training for business than we used to do in departments of economics seems to me uncertain. Perhaps
economics would be better for those students who have
the aspirations and the qualifications for administrative
work; certainly our business students would find better
opportunities to fit into some sort of job quickly. Most
of my graduates of years ago seem to me to be doing
extraordinarily well, better than I can easily imagine
most of our present students are likely to do.

## The Prostitution of American Education

But this is not the real point at issue. Even if we
assumed that our business-trained graduates w e r e
wanted in business and that they were likely to achieve
great wealth, we cannot say that this is what our
country needs. Our business is doing very well. I think
American business is the most efficient in the world.
Goods pour from our assembly lines in such a flood that
we are forced to work overtime to consume them to
prevent them from piling up and bringing a depression.
Of course, it never occurs to anyone that we might work
less at producing and at consuming and h a v e n o
depression.

The need is for better economic and political understanding, for the wisdom to save our civilized life.
With the growing complexity and integration of the
economy, the broad view of economics is more and
more needed; but in our universities we turn from that
to the narrow specialization for profits, turn to the training of minions for business. Needing desperately a
more enlightened and less fascistic class of businessmen,
we devote our energies and public funds to training
narrowly efficient businessmen who are not, indeed,
greatly needed and, if needed, should perhaps be trained
at the expense of self-supporting business. Business
should be not only "business-managed and taxpaying,"
but it should be self-supporting.

I confess to some doubt as to the measure of economic enlightenment we develop in our students in
economics. Many of them are devoid of intellectual
interest, being the natural product of our American environment; some of them have scarcely the intellectual
capacity to understand as elusive a study as economics;
few of them have any inclination to apply themselves

to anything that resembles work after the arduous functions of fraternity management and athletic rooting and raring have been attended to. When I talk to some of our economics or business graduates a few years after they leave us and get a few pungent remarks about the army of damn communists in Washington and a few questions about the football team and the new coaches and then an awkward and vacuous silence, I realize that these boys have not treasured the great truths that we so lavishly threw at them and that only by immaculate conception could they possibly get a new one. Like Professor Clay, I am convinced that the average worker is a more intelligent citizen than the average university graduate and that we might train our students better if we got them jobs in the industrial assembly line rather than in our academic assembly line. Yet we must do what we can, contenting ourselves with modest results lest in despair we decide on suicide as the logical end of the teacher's career. Certainly we might teach them more economics if we try to teach that, than we will if we try to teach them something else; and social intelligence is what we need.

On the other hand, there may be wisdom in some of our business school graduates. Social wisdom, intellectual interest, generosity and balance, these are to some extent natural qualities which, together with home influences, have perhaps more influence on the social outlook than college training; and, of course, most schools of business require some work in economics—as much as the students and the public will stand for. A few of our business students are intelligent citizens. Yet the mine-run of business school graduates consists of largely uneducated and uneducable men and women.

### The Prostitution of American Education

Our schools of business are not the only vocational schools that have been created, and we of academic circles have not been responsible for most of them. University presidents, some of them uninterested in education in any proper sense of that term, have had to measure their academic progress by the number of new schools they could set up and the number of new deans they could anoint and take out of teaching. So our university campuses are cluttered up with vocational and trade schools, each dedicated to the guidance of ignorant and ambitious young men and women in the great art and science of doing something practical for their personal advancement in matters economic and temporal.

Each school must, of course, have a dean; and most deans must have a retinue of assistant deans, accessory deans, accomplice deans and secretaries, with labyrinths of offices and with all the humming machinery that marks office efficiency in America. This vast aggregation of administrative paraphernalia and personnel meets all the requirements of worth, beauty, dignity and holiness according to the American tradition. It represents machinery, and Americans love machines —steam, electric, internal combustion, atomic and educational. Machinery *does* things. Furthermore, it absorbs funds and reduces the amount of educational work done and so builds up public support for the universities so that more machinery can be installed.

Nevertheless, the proliferation of schools and deans presents some serious problems. When the administrative machinery absorbs too much of the university income, it may be difficult to hire even enough teachers to provide the customary educational façade or it may be necessary to hire the teachers that the better-financed high schools do not want. The army of deans in some institutions presents a serious campus traffic hazard, and inter-dean rivalries and jurisdictional disputes sometimes approach the dignity of civil war.

The grotesque elephantiasis of schools and administrative machinery begets a fantastic proliferation of courses which tend to multiply by a sort of Malthusian compulsion. For this, we professors are partly responsible. When a school is established, the professors must, of course, build up a curriculum of specialized courses to train the students to do specific tasks, enough courses to cover every conceivable movement that the graduates will ever make, for it is always assumed that the students couldn't learn to sneeze unless they had a course in the process. Here our schools of business are not the worst offenders. Schools of education are far worse—witness the 1,000 courses in education in one of our large universities. But schools of business have a similar case of curricular obesity, and the offerings are not impressive or entrancingly interesting.

Some of the deans are not employed in managing and deploying faculties or "staffs"—"staff" is the common term for an aggregation or summation of professors —but have mostly police and supervisory functions, guarding student morals—student morals, like southern womanhood, are extraordinarily fragile and need constant attention—supervising student radical, humorous and pornographic publications and student behavior generally. For these functions there are usually deans of both men and women, although one dean should really be sufficient for this function since, of course, moral problems are usually bisexual. Then there are deans—perhaps called by other names—of health, research, social and religious activities, financial affairs, housing problems, and coordinate with deans, coaches, psychiatrists, marriage counselors, and generals and admirals and strings of orderlies following them to carry their packages and hold their stirrups while mounting. The modern university is an extraordinarily inclusive and cosmopolitan institution, somewhat on the model of a chain drug store.

If students study or the public reads some of the books currently excreted by some of the publishers, I believe I can understand why social ignorance is the American tradition. Here are some of the books: *Let's Sell!, How to Use Your Selling Power, Secrets of Closing Sales, Tested Sentences That Sell, How to Develop Profitable Ideas, How to Live and Work Successfully With People in Business, How to Hold an Audience Without a Rope*, etc., etc. *How to Make Friends and Influence People* is, of course, the towering landmark in American imbecility and hypocrisy, but I do not know whether it ever served as a textbook. *Sizzlemanship* is a more recent work, inspiring in the same way. Such fodder affords a growing proportion of the reading of many people in and out of college. It is not surprising that we botch our public affairs.

Too much and too poor. Too much and *consequently* too poor. Most college administrators, and a few professors as well, appear to believe that the number of courses measures the greatness of the college. The truth appears to be that once a modest number of good courses are offered, additional courses can raise the average only if they are better than those already given. If they are worse—as they usually are—they lower the average. In economic jargon, only when the marginal quality curve lies above the average quality line does the average quality curve slope up. The truth is, really, that much of the work in all schools, including the college of liberal arts, is poor, thin, desiccated, not worth the time of a mummy. A 30 to 50 per cent cut in the offerings of most schools would raise the quality of our education. I noted recently that in one of our great universities, 12 courses in copper hammering were being taught by, I presume, the professor of copper hammering; a dozen courses in weaving were given; and in the extension department, offerings included courses in ballroom dancing, advanced ballroom dancing, contract bridge, advanced contract bridge and a course in lead-wiping—whatever that means. In another large university I see a course in "ushering in church." Yes, these courses were being offered. I swear it on my sword.

We have not only spawned courses in the schools of business, we have concocted curricula in combination with other schools to give every student just exactly what he wants—but not an education. For a hypothetical illustration let us assume that an enterprising young American decides that he wants to be a salesman of aluminum ware and asks for special training. We call in deans and department heads from all over the campus and after a few days or weeks of deliberation decide on a curricular goulash which includes a dab of mining engineering—because of course the bauxite must be mined—a pinch of chemistry, a spoonful of strength of materials, and courses in accounting, marketing, salesmanship, psychology of salesmanship and advertising; but this won't fully equip him for his life of service so

we may develop some new courses: history of metals
with special reference to aluminum, aluminum and the
development of home industries, aluminum in its social
aspects, aluminum and foreign trade problems, aluminum and capitalism and, most important of all, aluminum and communism. We do all this on the prevalent
theory that the student will need very special training,
can't learn anything except in a course, and naturally
doesn't want an education. Very likely our efforts will
prove to be wasted because he may decide after all that
he would rather sell stocks or groceries or drive a truck.

Education isn't improving. In spite of all the money
we spend on convenient classrooms and seminar rooms
and laboratories and recreation rooms, a student has
less chance of getting an education than he had 50
years ago when most of the few courses were educational and worth taking. In most universities every new
school set up in the last 50 years and many of the courses
added have meant a degradation of our educational
standards.

Perhaps some of you may remember that Jesus
never condemned the fallen woman; and taking my
cue from Him, I do not blame any one for the sorry
prostitution of education to vocational ends. No more
indeed than I would blame the musk ox for growing long
wool, the fishes for developing fins, the rabbits for
having a high birth rate: it is a question of survival.
Our business school deans are honorable men, not a
few of them real scholars working hard to keep standards up and protect their schools from too much de-
bauchery by outside interests. The Americans a r e
uninterested in education or even regard it with sus-

picion, and they want jobs and money, and we have adapted ourselves to the forces operating in our environment. As the great Calvin Coolidge once said: "The business of America is business." It is one of the tragedies of our lives that we are under public suspicion as intellectuals—therefore subversives—while as a matter of fact we are employees in the service of business quite like plumbers and truck drivers. Furthermore, if we had not our vocational and trade schools, we should have so few students in our universities that again we could not do much teaching of the social sciences.

We teachers don't do much educational work anyhow. Let us be honest about it. If we did, America would surely not be a madhouse. The real teachers are the men of substance who control the newspapers, magazines, movies and the radio and television programs. A recent bulletin of the A.D.A. points out that in Wisconsin "McCarthy carried every county in the state where all or a majority of the newspapers supported him, or refused to expose his contemptible conduct or stood silent. But he lost every county in the state in which either a daily paper or a labor weekly fought him with the facts." McCarthyism is the fruit of newspaper education, and lunacy is the requirement for a degree. (I hope I am not offending any of the sons of our great sister state who may be loyal to their present type of statesmanship.) But this points the way to reform. Let us recognize that the princes of solvency who control the doors to the public mind are the really important teachers, and let us require of them the same training that we require of the less important flunkies in academic work—nothing less than a Ph.D. in the social sciences. Let us set this as the minimum requirement for running a newspaper or operating any business engaged in forming the public mind.

This would tend to provide the enlightenment needed in our educational work, but it would not provide the incentive to use that intelligence in the public interest, and I suggest that in addition we should require that journalists be accorded the tenure guaranteed in reputable universities—the freedom to write and publish the truth as they see it. Most journalists, like most professors, are intelligent people, the leading journalists brilliant; and if we could free them from the brass shackles of business they could do a generally respectable job of education. If they were free, furthermore, an even better class of talent would go into journalism.

Here then, ladies and gentlemen, I offer you the solution to our most serious problem—the problem of American political illiteracy and madness. Columbus discovered America; Copernicus discovered the solar system; Pasteur discovered the cause of hydrophobia; Lord Keynes discovered the New Economics and the cure for depressions; I now lay before you the remedy for public ignorance and mass insanity, the means of preserving civilization. Accept it with my compliments. When I began this paper I had no idea I should be able to accomplish so much. It is true that it may be difficult to secure the cooperation of the newspapers in presenting it to the people and difficult then to put into practice, but that is something for practical men to work out. With all our American machinery, know-how, vigor, pep, punch, push, pull and practical precocity, that should not be impossible.

# A LETTER TO
# SENATOR DOUGLAS

*A letter written to Senator Paul Douglas of Illinois on
the occasion of the "give away " of off-shore oil lands.
It was placed in the Congressional Record, May 7,
1952.*

Dear Senator Douglas:

I understand that in pursuit of efficiency, economy,
integrity, private enterprise and Americanism and in a
valiant effort to stem the socialist tide in our country,
Congress is distributing the federal assets to deserving
citizens of the Republic; and I wish you would keep
me in mind for my share of these assets. Specifically,
I would like to get some oil—I believe my share is
about 100 barrels (just have the oil shipped to me by
freight or truck)—and a hydroelectric plant and a national park, or if that is impracticable, a national forest
with a reasonable amount of grazing land.

As to the national park, I do not want a large
national park but only one of modest proportions. My
preference would be for Yosemite, Crater Lake or
Glacier Park. I would not care too much for a park
as large as Yellowstone or Grand Canyon because I
doubt if my income as professor would enable me to

develop and maintain it unless you could get me a fairly big hydroelectric plant. But I would not care too much for a cave park for I like to be above ground as much as possible for the benefit of the sunshine on my rheumatism.

If other scoundrels should beat me to the national parks, I would not complain if I could get a nice national forest—Dixie National Forest in Utah or the San Juan National Forest in Colorado or the Kaibab Forest in Arizona—a forest with plenty of trees to cut, some deer and bears to kill and a good view. In any case I should have a few thousand acres of grazing land near so I could keep a few cows and sheep and goats. Does the government provide cows and sheep and goats?

If the Congress decides to distribute federal buildings, I wish you would try to get the White House for me. I would even be able and glad, if necessary, to pay the same proportion of value that the corporations pay when they buy federal plants. I would really prefer the White House to the Capitol or the Pentagon for my wants are simple, being just a farm boy turned professor. My wife could rent out a few rooms for a modest revenue. I really need the White House very badly; but if you can't get it for me, please try to get me an embassy or a good post-office building. I could get by with that but not very comfortably.

If only the basement remnants of federal assets are given to Democrats, could you perhaps get me a harbor or a navigable river or a lighthouse or perhaps a battle cruiser or airplane carrier? An airplane carrier would be very useful for summer vacations. I would not care for a big airplane because I couldn't drive it very well, and I suppose it may be needed in the war.

[ 242 ]

## A *Letter to Senator Douglas*

I realize that you are only a Democrat, and I confess that I am only a Democrat too, although I am registered as a Republican because Democrats are regarded as subversives in Kansas. But I live in the President's own state, and I voted for Alf Landon in 1936. I have many Republican relatives; and I, myself, have a modest investment in several large Republican corporations. When the executor distributes the federal assets, does he give about equal amounts to each party as in some committee memberships or does he give all the assets to Republicans?

It is a delicate matter to mention, particularly to a man of your widely known punctiliousness with regard to senatorial proprieties, but I will, of course, be glad to pay the 5 per cent customary in past corrupt Democratic administrations or the 10 per cent of the present economy and reform administration.

Now, Senator Douglas, I am really anxious to get a little chunk of federal property, and I am even more anxious to do my generous part in stemming the tide of socialism in America. I hope you will be able to help me for old times' sake and for the sake of the country and freedom and democracy and private ownership and initiative.

Very sincerely yours,
John Ise

38957